Indoor Gardening Essentials

The Complete Guide to Growing Plants Inside Your Home

Taylor Mason

Table of Contents

INTRODUCTION 6

CHAPTER I: Understanding Indoor Gardening 7

Definition and scope..7

History and evolution of indoor gardening 11

Popularity and trends in indoor gardening 14

CHAPTER II: Planning Your Indoor Garden 17

Assessing your space..17

Determining light availability and quality 19

Choosing the right plants for your environment...........22

Basic Indoor garden design principles 24

CHAPTER III: Essential Tools and Supplies 27

Pots and Containers 27

Soil Types and Amendments 29

Watering Equipment 32

Lightning Solutions (natural and artificial) 34

Fertilizers and plant nutrients 37

Miscellaneous tools (pruners, stakes, supports) 39

CHAPTER IV: Choosing the Right Plants 42

Low Lights vs. High-light plant................................. 42

Easy-care plants for beginners 44

Specialty plants (herbs, vegetables, tropical, succulents)

.... 47

CHAPTER V: Plant Care Basics 50

Watering schedules and techniques 50

Feeding and fertilizing 53

Pruning and trimming 55

Repotting and transplanting 57

CHAPTER VI: Troubleshooting Common Issues 61

Identifying pests and diseases 61

Managing plant stress 63

Dealing with common problems (yellow leaves, root rot, etc.) 66

CHAPTER VII: Lighting for Indoor Plants 70

Understanding light requirements 70

Types of grow lights 72

Setting up and maintaining lighting systems 75

CHAPTER VIII: Temperature and Humidity Control 78

Ideal temperature ranges for different plants 78

Humidity management techniques 81

Using Humidifiers and dehumidifiers 83

CHAPTER IX: Air Circulation and Ventilation 86

Importance of air movement 86

Setting up fans and ventilation systems 89

Preventing mold and mildew 91

CHAPTER X: Growing Herbs Indoors 94

Best herbs for indoor gardening 94

Planting and care tips 96

Harvesting and using fresh herbs 99

CHAPTER XI: Indoor Vegetable Gardening 103

Choosing the right vegetables................................... 103

Container gardening techniques 105

Pollination and harvesting 108

CHAPTER XII: Growing Exotic and Tropical Plants......... 111

Understanding exotic plant needs 111

Creating microclimates 113

Special care tips for tropical plants 117

CHAPTER XIII: Hydroponic and Aquaponic Systems 120

Basics of hydroponics... 120

Setting up a hydroponic garden 123

Introduction to aquaponics 127

CHAPTER XIV: Vertical Gardening and Space Optimization

.. 130

Vertical gardening techniques................................... 130

Choosing the right vertical gardening system 132

Maximizing small spaces 134

CHAPTER XV: Creating a Green Indoor Oasis 137

Designing aesthetically pleasing plant displays 137

Integrating plants into home décor 139

Maintaining a balanced indoor ecosystem 141

CONCLUSION 144

INTRODUCTION

"Indoor Gardening Essentials: The Complete Guide to Growing Plants Inside Your Home." This book is the best resource for anybody interested in bringing their love of gardening indoors, whether an experienced gardener wishing to bring their passion inside or a total novice ready to experience the joys of raising green life in your home. There is nothing quite like indoor gardening to combine aesthetics, peace of mind, and usefulness. It can turn any house into a verdant haven and let you grow beautiful, lush plants all year round, regardless of the weather outside.

The following pages contain everything you need to start and maintain a successful indoor garden. We begin with the fundamentals, offering essential tools and supplies and assisting you in selecting the appropriate plants. You will learn about your plants' requirements, from light and water to nutrients and humidity, and how to meet them. Advanced techniques such as propagation, trimming, and plant display design are also discussed to ensure that your indoor garden is both aesthetically beautiful and healthy.

Whether you want to cultivate simple succulents, exotic topicals, or edible plants, this guide will help you achieve this with expert recommendations, helpful advice, and motivational ideas. Take the plunge and start your indoor gardening adventure, turning your house into a verdant paradise that offers happiness, elegance, and fresh air.

CHAPTER I
Understanding Indoor Gardening

Definition and scope

As old as civilization, indoor gardening has come a long way from a fundamental need to a well-liked and fulfilling pastime. This section explores the definition and application of indoor gardening, emphasizing its diverse character and its many advantages to both novices and enthusiasts.

Fundamentally, indoor gardening is growing plants indoors—in offices, residences, or any other confined environment. This method involves cultivating many plants, including tiny fruit trees, herbs, vegetables, decorative houseplants, and blooming species. The main attraction of indoor gardening is that it allows people to enjoy the beauty and health benefits of plants within, independent of their outdoor surroundings. Whether you live in a suburban house or an apartment in the city, indoor gardening allows you to create a green haven.

The field of indoor gardening is vast and adaptable, with various approaches and strategies appropriate for multiple plant species and available areas. Plants are typically cultivated in pots or other containers filled with soil or specialty potting mixes in traditional soil-based gardening. On the other hand, new technologies have brought about creative methods like aquaponics, aeroponics, and hydroponics. These soilless techniques provide effective and compact indoor plant growth options. For example, aeroponics employs mist to provide nutrients to the roots, while hydroponics grows plants in a nutrient-rich water solution. In aquaponics, fish excrement is used to supply nutrients to the plants, combining hydroponics and aquaculture.

Choosing the appropriate plants for the interior environment based on their unique characteristics is one of the most essential parts of indoor gardening. Which plants will flourish inside depends mainly on several factors, including temperature, humidity, availability of light, and available space. Low-light plants like pothos, ZZ plants, and snake plants are perfect for locations with little natural light. However, plants like cacti and succulents perform better on windowsills or under grow lights because they need robust and direct sunshine. Maintaining the health and vigor of indoor plants requires understanding these requirements.

A key element of indoor gardening is light regulation. Although natural light is the ideal source for plant growth, it is frequently insufficient, particularly inside, where windows may require lighter during the day. Gardeners typically add artificial illumination as a supplement to remedy this. Grow lights are available in various forms, including high-intensity discharge (HID), LED, and fluorescent lights. These lights can replicate natural sunshine and offer the spectrum required for photosynthesis. When encouraging healthy development and flowering, indoor gardeners must pay close attention to the positioning and length of light exposure.

There are also notable differences in watering techniques between gardening indoors and outside. To avoid problems such as overwatering or underwatering, indoor plants usually need more regulated and exact watering regimens. The watering frequency depends on several factors, including the type of plant, container size, and ambient humidity. For example, compared to tropical plants that require constant moisture in the soil, succulents, and cacti require less regular watering because they store water in their leaves. It is essential to keep an eye on soil moisture levels and be aware of the unique requirements of every kind of plant to maintain ideal hydration.

Indoor plants need the proper nutrients, in addition to light and water, to thrive. Fertilizers are frequently used in indoor gardening to supply the nutrients that potting soil might need to provide in sufficient amounts. Fertilizers are available in liquid, granular, and slow-release formulations, each with unique advantages. A well-balanced fertilization strategy customized to the plants' individual requirements guarantees healthy growth and colorful leaves.

Even without getting into the technical details, indoor gardening has many positive effects that improve quality of life. The enhancement of indoor air quality is one of the most enormous benefits. Numerous indoor plants, including Boston ferns, peace lilies, and spider plants, are well-known for their capacity to release oxygen into the air and filter contaminants, thus fostering a healthier living space. This natural air filtration can improve respiratory health by lowering the levels of dangerous compounds like formaldehyde, benzene, and trichloroethylene.

The benefits of indoor gardening extend to mental health. Having greenery around and caring for plants might help lessen stress, anxiety, and depressive symptoms. Studies have shown that engaging with plants can reduce blood pressure and foster a feeling of peace and relaxation.

Indoor gardening has become a healing hobby for many individuals, giving them a respite from technology and a way to reconnect with the natural world.

Furthermore, indoor gardening encourages self-sufficiency and sustainability. Producing edible plants indoors, such as fruits, vegetables, and herbs, lessens the need for store-bought food, which frequently has large carbon footprints from packing and shipping. Produce grown organically has fewer chemicals and pesticides, making it fresher and tastier. This change to more environmentally friendly living methods promotes a greater appreciation for the food we eat and leads to an eco-friendly lifestyle.

It is necessary to recognize indoor gardening's aesthetic appeal. Any interior space is enhanced and made more pleasant by the beauty and elegance that houseplants bring. Indoor plants can be used as central points in spaces or as a complement to various decor styles, whether placed in fashionable pots, hanging baskets, or vertical gardens. The array of plant varieties, forms, and hues opens up countless creative options for creating inside gardens that express individual preferences and aesthetics.

To sum up, indoor gardening is a flexible and rewarding hobby with many advantages. The benefits of indoor gardening are numerous and varied, from enhancing mental health and air quality to fostering sustainability and adding aesthetic value. To create a successful indoor garden, one must comprehend the basic principles of indoor gardening, such as plant selection, light control, watering, and feeding. Indoor gardening is becoming increasingly popular as more individuals adopt this habit, turning their homes into verdant retreats and encouraging a closer bond with the natural world.

History and evolution of indoor gardening

With a rich and varied history spanning ages and continents, indoor gardening is the art of growing plants indoors. Its evolution has been characterized by significant advances in science, technology, and culture that have influenced how people cultivate and value indoor plants. This section examines the development of indoor gardening over time, emphasizing significant turning points and inventions that have aided in its rise to prominence.

Early attempts to cultivate plants indoors were driven by a fascinating blend of practicality and aesthetics, rooted in the ancient cultures. For instance, the affluent Egyptians, with a sense of wonder, grew plants in pots in their courtyards and homes, integrating nature into their architectural landscape and showcasing their status. Similarly, the ancient Romans, with a curiosity for horticulture and garden design, adorned their atriums and courtyards with potted plants, a testament to their love for nature.

During the European Renaissance, when curiosity in science, art, and travel was piqued, the idea of indoor gardening continued to develop. Wealthy nobility and aristocracy hired glasshouse builders to build orangeries, which were expansive glass buildings that shielded exotic flora like citrus trees from bitter winter weather. These orangeries served as an early example of a greenhouse, using glass to create a controlled space ideal for growing plants. The emergence of these frameworks revealed a growing comprehension of the significance of temperature, light, and humidity in indoor plant culture.

Significant progress in indoor gardening was made in the 18th and 19th centuries due to the Industrial Revolution and Enlightenment scientific discoveries. Plant transportation and cultivation were transformed when Dr. Nathaniel Bagshaw Ward created the Wardian case in the early 1800s. The safe long-distance transportation of fragile plants in this sealed glass case made the exchange of plant species between continents possible. Additionally, the Wardian case offered a controlled environment that shielded plants from pollutants and pests, enabling hobbyists to grow a more excellent range of indoor plants.

In Europe and North America during the Victorian era, indoor gardening gained popularity among the middle and higher classes. At this time, an increasing number of greenhouses and conservatories were attached to private residences, where exotic plants gathered from all over the world were on show and could be appreciated. The growth of botanical gardens and the publication of gardening books and magazines, which spread knowledge about plant care and cultivation methods, contributed to the Victorian era's love of botany and horticulture. During this period, indoor gardening was a pastime and a representation of sophistication and higher learning.

The 20th century saw further indoor gardening developments due to lifestyle changes and technological breakthroughs. The invention of climate control systems and electric lighting made it possible to create artificial habitats that could sustain plant growth all year round, independent of the outside weather. A more effective and efficient light source for indoor plants was made available with the development of fluorescent lighting in the middle of the 20th century, encouraging healthier growth and a more comprehensive range of plant choices. Thanks to these technical developments, indoor gardening became more widely available and a well-liked pastime for people from all walks of life, not just the wealthy.

The environmental movement and rising ecological consciousness in the second half of the 20th century significantly influenced the development of indoor gardening. Interest in cultivating fruits, vegetables, and herbs indoors has grown as people seek more sustainable living and self-sufficiency. Since they effectively use space and resources, soilless plant production techniques like hydroponics and aquaponics have grown in popularity. These techniques made it possible for city people with little outdoor area to grow food, which fueled the growth of urban agriculture.

The advent of the internet and the digital era has brought a new sense of community and shared passion to indoor gardening. Social media and online platforms have united indoor gardening enthusiasts, fostering the exchange of advice, knowledge, and ideas. Online tools such as tutorial videos, discussion boards, and plant care manuals have democratized information and skill access, making it easier for beginners to embark on their indoor gardening journey. The advancement of smart gardening technologies has also enhanced the indoor gardening experience, making it more accessible and enjoyable for all.

Indoor gardening is a dynamic and varied practice that is still developing today. It includes various techniques and methods, including high-tech vertical farms, conventional soil-based gardening, and biophilic design, which incorporates plants into architectural spaces to enhance well-being and foster a sense of connection with nature. Numerous considerations, such as the desire for aesthetic improvement, better air quality, mental health advantages, and sustainable living practices, have contributed to the popularity of indoor gardening.

In summary, the development and history of indoor gardening reveal a nuanced interaction between scientific, technological, and cultural factors. Indoor gardening has evolved to meet shifting requirements and tastes, from its earliest days in Egypt and Rome to the modern, highly developed intelligent gardens. This long-standing custom has improved people's living environments and increased their enjoyment of nature by bringing it closer to them.

As time passes, indoor gardening is expected to maintain its innovative and expanding history while becoming an increasingly significant part of urban living, sustainability, and individual well-being.

Popularity and trends in indoor gardening

With the help of new technologies, changing social mores, and an increasing understanding of the advantages of bringing plants indoors, indoor gardening has seen a meteoric rise in popularity in the last several years. This section looks at current trends influencing indoor gardening and the circumstances that led to its popularity.

People's increased concern for sustainability and well-being is essential to indoor gardening's rising well-being. As people become more aware of their health and environmental effects, indoor gardening is a way to foster well-being and connect with nature within the limits of urban living. It has been demonstrated that indoor plants improve mood, stress levels, and air quality, all of which contribute to happier, healthier homes. Moreover, cultivating fresh fruits, vegetables, or herbs indoors with indoor gardening enables people to lead more self-sufficient and sustainable lifestyles.

Technological improvements have significantly fueled the rise in popularity of indoor gardening. The emergence of LED grow lights, hydroponic systems, and intelligent gardening tools has revolutionized the accessibility and effectiveness of indoor plant growth. Compared to conventional lighting sources, LED grow lights use less energy and produce less heat while providing the whole spectrum of light required for plant growth. With hydroponic systems, plants can grow directly in nutrient-rich water solutions, negating soil needs and potentially producing larger yields and faster growth rates. By giving users access to real-time information and warnings regarding soil moisture, light levels, and temperature, innovative gardening tools like plant monitors and automated watering systems make it simpler for people to take care of their plants.

The rise in popularity of indoor gardening can also be attributed to social media and online groups, which offer forums for enthusiasts to exchange advice, concepts, and motivation. Many videos and pictures of gorgeous indoor gardens and inventive plant arrangements can be found on social media sites like YouTube, Pinterest, and Instagram. These resources might encourage people to start their indoor gardening projects. People can interact with like-minded people, ask questions, and seek guidance from seasoned growers through online forums and clubs devoted to indoor gardening, promoting community and camaraderie.

The current indoor gardening trends show that sustainability, self-sufficiency, and beautiful design are becoming increasingly important. Growing edible plants, like herbs, veggies, and microgreens, is becoming increasingly popular among indoor gardeners to lower their environmental impact and reduce their need for produce from stores. Living walls and vertical gardens are becoming more and more common as compacting options for city people trying to fit as much greenery as possible into limited areas. In addition to adding visual interest, these vertical layouts increase the space available for growing plants and enhance the air quality within.

Another design movement affecting indoor gardening is biophilic design, which aims to bring natural features into constructed surroundings. To create environments supporting productivity and well-being, interior designers and architects are increasingly adding plants and greenery into residential and business spaces. Indoor plants are used in living rooms, business atriums, hotel lobbies, and private balconies and living rooms to soften architectural lines, lower noise levels, and create livable, comfortable environments for residents.

In conclusion, as more people look for ways to improve their living conditions, health, and sustainability, indoor gardening is becoming increasingly popular. Social media, technological developments, and shifting public perceptions of sustainability and well-being have all helped indoor gardening become a more well-liked and fulfilling pastime. Growing edible plants, vertical gardening, and biophilic design are becoming increasingly popular indoor gardening ideas, emphasizing sustainability, self-sufficiency, and beautiful design. As indoor gardening develops further, it will always be a beloved hobby for people who want to incorporate nature's beauty and health advantages into their homes.

CHAPTER II
Planning Your Indoor Garden

Assessing your space

The first stage in designing an indoor garden is making a detailed assessment of the available area. It's crucial to ensure your gardening efforts are sustainable and prosperous. This section discusses the value of evaluating your indoor garden space and offers helpful advice on making the most of it.

Planning an indoor garden starts with assessing the space's physical attributes, such as its dimensions, design, and surrounding circumstances. The size of the space or room where you plan to establish your indoor garden should be considered, along with any architectural elements like windows, doors, and ventilation systems. Evaluate the quantity of daylight that reaches the area during the day and any potential artificial lighting sources. Light's kind and intensity significantly impact plant growth and will help you choose the plants that will thrive in your indoor space.

Next, assess the indoor space's climatic factors, such as humidity, air movement, and temperature. Specific temperature and humidity ranges are ideal for indoor plant growth. Therefore, monitoring these parameters and making any required modifications is critical to produce the perfect growing environment. Consider anything that could alter the temperature and humidity levels, such as air vents, heating and cooling systems, and drafts. Assuring that your indoor space has enough ventilation is essential for avoiding problems like mold, mildew, and pest infestations.

After evaluating your interior space's environmental and physical aspects, consider how to utilize it for gardening best. Determine which parts of your room get the lightest, such as windows facing south or open spaces next to skylights. Herbs, vegetables, and flowering plants that require light are best planted in these sunny places. Consider adding artificial grow lights to places with insufficient natural light to help supply the light spectrum needed for plant growth. Energy-efficient and adaptable LED grow lights can be tailored to match the unique requirements of various plants.

Think about how to maximize vertical space in your indoor garden in addition to light issues. Vertical gardening maximizes the use of available space by using walls, shelves, or hanging planters to raise plants upwards. Vertical gardens may bring visual interest to any indoor space and are especially well-suited for tiny or tight spaces. Installing wall-mounted planters, trellises, or shelving units can help you create a vertical garden display that blends in well with your current interior design and uplifts the atmosphere of your room.

It's crucial to consider the practical aspects of plant care and upkeep while designing your indoor garden. Select plants appropriate for your degree of gardening experience and the indoor environment. Succulents, cacti, and air plants are low-maintenance plants great for novices or busy people who need more time or money to give their plants intensive care. Alternatively, if you're an accomplished gardener searching for a challenge, consider experimenting with more exotic or demanding plant species that call for particular upkeep guidelines.

Lastly, when designing your area, remember to consider the beauty of your indoor garden. Think about how plants, vases, and accent pieces enhance your interior space's overall style and atmosphere. Select containers that blend in with your current design, and for added visual flair, think about using natural materials like wood, ceramic, or terracotta. Try experimenting with different plant configurations, hues, and textures to produce an eye-catching indoor garden that expresses your aesthetic and improves the atmosphere of your home.

In conclusion, the first step in designing your indoor garden is to carefully evaluate the space you have available as well as the surrounding circumstances. By carefully considering these aspects and choosing plants, lighting, and layout, you can design a vibrant indoor garden that adds beauty, health, and energy to your house. A successful and joyful gardening experience can be achieved by careful planning and deliberate consideration of your interior area, regardless of skill level.

Determining light availability and quality

Light availability and quality determination are important parts of indoor gardening. As the main source of energy for plant growth and development, this section discusses the significance of evaluating the amount and quality of light in interior environments and offers helpful advice on how to provide the best possible growing conditions for indoor plants.

Light quality relates to the range and intensity of light wavelengths, whereas light availability refers to the quantity of light that reaches a specific location inside an interior environment. These two criteria determine the plants that will grow well, and which ones will flourish in a given environment.

Knowing the natural illumination in your indoor location is the first step toward evaluating light availability. Keep an eye out for any structures that can obscure sunlight, such as surrounding buildings, trees, or other structures, as well as the positioning and orientation of the windows.

North-facing windows receive the least direct sunshine during the day, while south-facing windows often receive the most. East and west-facing windows come in second and third place to south-facing windows. Observe how light streams through windows and varies over the day and seasons. It will enable you to pinpoint the areas that receive the most even light distribution.

Think about the availability of artificial lighting sources as an additional light source that can complement or replace natural sunlight. Grow lights are an excellent choice for indoor gardening since they are specifically made to deliver the entire spectrum of light wavelengths required for photosynthesis. Energy-efficient and adaptable, LED grow lights let you modify the light's spectrum and intensity to suit the requirements of various plants. Popular solutions for indoor gardening are fluorescent and HID (high-intensity discharge) lights, which provide reasonably priced ways to give plants extra lighting.

After determining how much light is available, you must decide how good the light is inside your space. Plants use the entire spectrum of light wavelengths natural sunlight produces for photosynthesis, including red, blue, and green. Different plants require different amounts of light to survive; some enjoy robust and direct sunshine, while others do well in less light. Knowing what light your plants need can help you decide where in your interior space to put them and what lighting fixtures would be best for their growth.

In addition, variables including uniformity, duration, and light intensity affect the quality of the light. Light brightness, expressed in foot-candles or lux, is light intensity. This brightness has an impact on plant growth and photosynthetic rate. While some plants can survive at lower light levels, most indoor plants need moderate to high light, usually between 1000 and 3000-foot candles. The length of the light exposure is also significant because plants require a minimum of hours of light per day to continue thriving. Most houseplants need 12 to 16 hours of light daily, though this could change based on the species and growth stage.

When evaluating light quality, uniformity of light distribution is an additional consideration. Plants that receive an unequal amount of light may grow and develop unevenly, becoming lanky or stunted. And guarantee uniform light distribution, plants should be positioned uniformly beneath lighting fixtures and rotated frequently to expose all sides to light. To distribute light more evenly around the space and bounce it off various surfaces, consider utilizing numerous light sources or reflective materials.

In conclusion, the key to successful indoor gardening is determining the availability and quality of light. You may establish an ideal habitat for plant growth and guarantee the health and vitality of your indoor plants by carefully evaluating the natural and artificial lighting conditions within your indoor area. A healthy indoor garden starts with knowing what your plants need in terms of light and creating the ideal lighting environment, whether growing herbs on a kitchen windowsill or creating a lush indoor jungle.

Choosing the right plants for your environment

A successful indoor garden depends on selecting the appropriate plants for your interior space. This section examines what to consider when choosing indoor plants and offers helpful advice on picking plants suitable for your particular setting.

The first step in selecting the ideal indoor plants is to evaluate the available space and the light, temperature, humidity, and other environmental factors. Assessing how much and what kind of natural light penetrates your indoor space during the day should be your first step. Consider the windows' position, the existence of any obstacles that could create shadows, and any artificial lighting you intend to utilize. Different plants require different amounts of light to survive; some enjoy robust and direct sunshine, while others do well in less light. Select indoor plants that will grow and develop healthily by being well-suited to the amount of light they receive.

Next, consider your indoor space's temperature and humidity levels, as these can also affect the health and vitality of your plants. Most indoor plants thrive in daytime temperatures between 65°F and 75°F and nighttime temperatures that are somewhat colder. Nonetheless, certain types of plants, such as those found in tropical regions, could need more humidity to flourish. If the air inside your home is dry and devoid of humidity, think about adding techniques to bring in more moisture, including utilizing a humidifier, setting up pebble trays with water underneath plants, or clustering plants to create a humid microclimate.

Another crucial factor to consider when selecting plants for your interior space is available space. Examine the inside area's available space and arrangement, taking note of the floor plan, tabletops, shelves, and hanging locations. Select plants that complement your area's size while considering each plant's mature size and growth tendencies. Though trailing or vining plants can be hung in baskets or on walls to maximize vertical space, compact, bushy plants are perfect for tabletops or tiny spaces. Use vertical gardening techniques like trellises or wall-mounted planters to maximize your limited space and design an eye-catching indoor garden show.

After evaluating your surroundings and available space, investigate plant species most suited to your requirements and preferences. Plants for your indoor garden should be chosen with growing habits, maintenance needs, and aesthetic appeal in mind. Succulents, cacti, and snake plants are low-maintenance plants that are great for novices or people with little time or gardening experience. These plants are adaptable for interior spaces since they can flourish in various lighting settings and are drought tolerant.

Consider using flowering plants or foliage plants with vivid foliage patterns and textures to bring color and variation to your indoor garden. Their vibrant blossoms, flowering plants like peace lilies, orchids, and African violets enliven indoor environments and lend beauty and elegance. Because of their eye-catching patterns and textures, leaf plants, including prayer plants, ferns, and calatheas, are famous for artistic indoor displays.

Apart from the distinct requirements of every type of plant, contemplate how several plants will work in harmony to form a harmonious indoor garden design. Play around with different arrangements of plants, pots, and accent pieces to design an aesthetically pleasing indoor garden that expresses your style and elevates the atmosphere of your home. Plants requiring similar care should be grouped to facilitate maintenance and watering tasks and ensure each plant receives the necessary care to thrive.

In conclusion, developing a healthy and flourishing indoor garden requires selecting the appropriate plants for your indoor space. By carefully considering your growing environment, available space, and personal taste, you can design a colorful and lovely indoor garden, adding beauty and delight to your house. A year-round indoor garden can be created with careful design and critical attention, regardless of gardening expertise level. With the right plants and care, you may reap the rewards of indoor gardening and create a verdant haven that elevates your indoor living area.

Basic Indoor garden design principles

Applying fundamental concepts of indoor garden design can create aesthetically pleasing and valuable interior environments that support plant health and well-being. This section examines the basic design concepts for indoor gardens and offers helpful advice on how to implement these concepts to create harmonious and aesthetically beautiful displays of indoor gardens.

Balance, or the distribution of visual weight within a space, is the fundamental rule of indoor garden design. In indoor gardens, balance is achieved by placing plants, containers, and accent pieces to foster harmony and balance. Symmetrical or asymmetrical layouts can be used to establish balance depending on the intended look and feel of the indoor garden. Place items equally on either side of a center axis to achieve symmetrical balance and a formal, organized appearance. In contrast, asymmetrical balance employs an unequal distribution of visual weight to generate visual intrigue and movement by arranging parts more organic and relaxedly.

Proportion, or the size and scale of plants, containers, and ornamental elements about one another and the entire space, is another crucial design concept for indoor gardens. In indoor garden displays, proportion ensures that all components blend harmoniously and contribute to coherence and harmony. Consider the scale of your area and choose items appropriate for the size of the room or area when selecting plants and containers for your indoor garden. Large plants or pots should not be crammed into the area or overpower it as this can make it appear congested and out of proportion. Instead, strive for a harmonious indoor garden by using a well-balanced selection of plants and containers that enhance one another.

Another fundamental design concept for indoor gardens is unity, which refers to the harmonious interplay of various components in a room. To produce a unified and aesthetically pleasing exhibit, indoor garden designers must carefully choose their plants, containers, and ornamental accents. Choose ones with comparable maintenance needs and aesthetic attributes to guarantee that your plants blend well together and have a cohesive appearance. Use coordinating color palettes, textures, and patterns to bring the indoor garden together and establish a feeling of continuity all around. Create a visually appealing, cohesive exhibit that improves the overall mood of your interior space by incorporating unity into your indoor garden design.

Rhythm and repetition, balance, proportion, and unity are significant design elements that enhance the overall beauty of indoor gardens. When components in a room, such as plants, containers, or decorative accents, are repeated, a sense of visual flow and movement is produced and known as rhythm. Create a sense of rhythm and movement that pulls the eye and adds visual interest to the indoor garden by repeating similar pieces throughout. To make an indoor garden exhibit that is both visually appealing and harmonious, use recurring patterns, shapes, or colors.

Another crucial component of indoor garden design is texture, which gives the area depth and visual appeal. To add depth and contrast to your indoor garden exhibit, use a range of textures, such as glossy, matte, rough, and smooth surfaces; plants with varying foliage textures, such as glossy topicals, fuzzy ferns, and smooth succulents, can be mixed and matched to create a visually stimulating indoor garden show. Decorative stones, pebbles, or driftwood are textural items that can be added to your indoor space to provide tactile appeal and improve the overall atmosphere.

Finally, when creating your indoor garden, keep the concepts of hierarchy and focal point in mind. An eye-catching feature or piece that acts as a visual anchor for the design is a focus point. To establish visual appeal and balance in the room, pick a central feature for your indoor garden, such as a vast statement plant, a stylish container, or a sculpture. Arrange your plants and ornamental accents in a way that makes a clear visual hierarchy and highlights the space's main focal points to create a sense of order and importance in your indoor garden show.

To sum up, fundamental concepts of indoor garden design are essential to designing aesthetically pleasing and valuable interior environments that support the health and welfare of plants. You may build a harmonic and visually beautiful indoor garden, improving the entire ambiance of your indoor area. These principles include balance, proportion, unity, rhythm, repetition, texture, focal point, and hierarchy. Applying these design concepts with careful thought will enable you to build an indoor garden that is beautiful and joyful all year round, regardless of your level of gardening knowledge.

CHAPTER III
Essential Tools and Supplies

Pots and Containers

In the realm of indoor gardening, the choice of pots and containers is not just a matter of aesthetics, but a crucial factor that can significantly impact the health and growth of your plants. These containers serve as more than just receptacles; they are key players in the overall design of your indoor space. This section delves into the importance of selecting the right pots and containers for your indoor plants, offering valuable insights and practical tips to help you make informed decisions that will enhance your interior design and promote healthy plant growth.

It's crucial to consider both form and function when choosing pots and containers for indoor plants. To serve a purpose, jars, and containers should have enough room for plant roots to spread out and flourish and enough drainage to avoid soggy soil and root rot. Select pots with bottom drainage holes to let excess water runoff, maintaining a balanced soil moisture level and preventing water buildup at the bottom of the container. Avoid pots with inadequate drainage or holes since they can cause overwatering and smothering of the roots, harming the plant's health.

When choosing containers for indoor plants, consider not only drainage but also the material of the pots and containers. Indoor plant containers are frequently made of terracotta, ceramic, plastic, metal, and fiberglass, each of which has advantages and disadvantages of its own. Because terracotta pots are airy and porous, air and moisture may freely circulate plant roots; nevertheless, frequent watering may be necessary because of their propensity to dry up rapidly. Although ceramic pots are solid and available in various hues and designs, they may also be bulky and brittle. Although plastic pots are inexpensive, lightweight, and simple to clean, their visual appeal may be lower than other materials. Although metal and fiberglass pots are weather-resistant and lightweight, they might not offer plant roots as much insulation as pots made of different materials. Nonetheless, they can be used both indoors and outdoors.

When choosing containers for indoor plants, consider not only the material and function but also the design and aesthetics of the pots and containers. Select pots that showcase your design choices and blend well with your interior decor. Consider elements like color, texture, shape, and size when choosing pots and containers. Also, pick containers that complement the interior design of your room. To give your indoor plant exhibit personality and visual intrigue, mix and match different designs of containers. Personalize pots and containers with painted patterns, textures, or other ornamental accents to add personality to your indoor garden.

Select pots that are the right size for the plants you intend to grow when it comes to pot size. Smaller plants can flourish in smaller containers, but larger plants need larger pots with more excellent space for root growth. To prevent soggy soil and root rot, do not use pots that are too big for your plants. In an identical vein, avoid using too-small pots since this might limit root growth and impede the growth and development of plants. To ensure sufficient root extension when repotting plants into larger containers, select pots with a diameter one to two inches greater than the existing pot.

Think about using hanging baskets, wall-mounted planters, or terrariums as alternate indoor plant containers in addition to conventional pots and containers. In order to maximize vertical area, hanging baskets can be fixed on walls or suspended from ceilings, making them perfect for trailing or vining plants. Wall-mounted planters are ideal for creating vertical garden displays and bringing visual interest to blank walls. Terrariums are self-contained ecosystems kept in glass pots. They offer little plants a distinctive and artistic display option, allowing you to make tiny indoor gardens.

Pots and containers are crucial components of indoor gardening because they are both valuable receptacles for plant development and ornamental accents that improve the interior design overall. Consider drainage, material, style, size, and substitute alternatives when choosing pots and containers for indoor plants. Select planters that showcase your particular flair, go well with your interior design, and encourage robust plant growth. You may build a colorful and lovely indoor garden exhibit that enhances the beauty and happiness of your home with careful thought and pot and container selection.

Soil Types and Amendments

Comprehending the many types of soil and their additives is crucial for practical indoor gardening. Soil establishes the basis for plant development and functions as a storehouse for nutrients, water, and oxygen. This section discusses the significance of different soil types and amendments for indoor gardening and offers helpful advice on selecting the best soil and nutrients for indoor plants.

To begin comprehending soil types, you must first become familiar with the fundamental elements of soil and how they contribute to plant growth. The soil components include organic matter, minerals, water, air, and microbes. These elements are essential to creating a wholesome and productive plant-growing environment. While organic matter, such as compost, humus, and decomposed plant matter, supplies nutrients and enhances soil structure and fertility, mineral particles, such as sand, silt, and clay, give soil stability and structure. In addition to beneficial microorganisms like bacteria and fungus that aid in the breakdown of organic matter and release of nutrients for plant uptake, water, and air are necessary for plant growth because they hydrate and oxygenate plant roots.

It's crucial to consider the unique requirements and needs of every type of plant when choosing soil for indoor plants. Certain plants are better suited for sandy, well-draining soils, while others do well in loamy, moisture-retentive soils. When selecting soil for indoor plants, consider elements such as plant species, watering frequency, and pot capacity. To avoid waterlogging and root rot, use a fast-draining soil mix for succulents and cacti of sandy or gritty elements like perlite, pumice, or coarse sand. To retain moisture and encourage healthy root growth, use a well-aerated potting mix with a high organic matter content, such as compost, peat moss, or coconut coir, for tropical plants and species that love dampness.

To enhance soil structure, fertility, and drainage, consider adding soil amendments and choosing the appropriate type of soil. Organic or inorganic materials are added to soil as soil amendments to improve its qualities and maximize plant development. Compost, aged manure, vermicompost, perlite, vermiculite, and organic fertilizers are common soil additions with unique advantages. Over time, soil structure and fertility are improved by adding vital plant nutrients to the soil through compost and aged manure, which are excellent organic matter and nutrient sources. Worm castings, also known as vermicompost, are a concentrated supply of organic matter, microorganisms that are good for plants, and nutrients that are rich in nutrients that earthworms generate.

Lightweight, porous minerals like perlite and vermiculite are frequently added to soil as soil amendments to enhance drainage and aeration. The lightweight, porous particles that make up perlite are formed by heating and expanding volcanic glass, which improves soil drainage and reduces compaction. Vermiculite is a naturally occurring mineral heated to a larger size. This process produces light, moisture-retentive particles that help retain soil moisture and provide plant roots oxygen. Perlite and vermiculite are frequently used in potting mixes to enhance soil structure and encourage strong root development.

To supply vital nutrients for plant growth, think about adding organic fertilizers to your indoor gardening regimen in addition to organic soil amendments. Compost tea, fish emulsion, seaweed extract, and bone meal are examples of organic fertilizers that offer plants a slow-release supply of nutrients that support good growth and development. Select organic fertilizers that are made especially for your plants' needs and appropriate for indoor use. Refrain from overfertilizing indoor plants, which may result in nutrient imbalances and problems with the plant's health. Instead, adhere to the suggested dosage guidelines and track plant development and reaction to ascertain when further fertilization is required.

To sum up, good indoor gardening requires a grasp of soil types and nutrients. Select the appropriate soil type for healthy and productive indoor plant growth and add soil amendments to enhance drainage, fertility, and soil structure. When choosing soil and additives, consider variables like plant species, watering frequency, and pot size. Ensure the goods you purchase are appropriate for the particular requirements of your plants. With correct soil management and upkeep, you may develop a flourishing indoor garden that infuses your interior area with beauty and life.

Watering Equipment

An integral part of indoor gardening, watering equipment is vital for preserving ideal soil moisture levels and encouraging strong plant development. This section explores the importance of watering tools for indoor gardening and provides helpful advice on choosing the best tools and methods for watering indoor plants.

Watering equipment is a broad category that includes a variety of implements and apparatuses intended to supply water properly and efficiently to indoor plants. Watering cans, watering wands, and spray bottles are the most basic watering tools; each has a distinct function and meets a demand for watering. With the help of these valuable instruments, gardeners may carefully and gently water their plants, ensuring that no soil or foliage is disturbed. One such item is a watering can. With long spouts for reaching deeply into pots and narrow apertures for regulated pouring, they are available in various sizes and styles. Watering wands are garden hose extension adapters that provide more reach and precise watering for hanging baskets, tall plants, and difficult-to-reach spots. Spray bottles are handy for spot-watering small plants with delicate foliage, misting plants, and applying foliar treatments.

Specialized watering tools, such as moisture meters, drip irrigation systems, and self-watering pots, can help automate and simplify the watering process for indoor plants in addition to essential tools. With built-in reservoirs that store water and wick moisture into the soil when needed, self-watering pots give plants a steady supply of water while lowering the need for human watering. With drip irrigation systems, water is delivered directly to plant roots through tubing, emitters, and timers, reducing water waste and guaranteeing effective water distribution. With portable moisture meters, gardeners may monitor and modify the watering frequency under the requirements of their plants and the surrounding conditions.

Considerations including plant species, pot size, and surrounding circumstances should be considered when choosing irrigation equipment for indoor plants. Different plants require different amounts of water; some like their soil to be continually moist, while others would rather the soil to dry out a little between waterings. Considering elements like soil type, drainage, and humidity levels, select watering tools and methods suitable for your plants' requirements. For instance, plants in soil that drains well need to be watered more frequently than those in heavier soil, and plants in low-humidity settings might benefit from routine misting to raise the moisture content surrounding leaves.

Consider the pot's material and size when choosing indoor plant watering equipment. Because they hold less soil and moisture than bigger pots, smaller pots, and containers must be watered more frequently. Select irrigation equipment with gentle watering capabilities and precise control to prevent overwatering or waterlogging small pots. When choosing watering equipment, consider the material of the pots and containers as well, as different materials have varied water retention qualities. For instance, plastic pots retain moisture better and need less frequent watering than terracotta pots, which are porous and absorbent and allow moisture to drain from the soil more quickly.

Maintaining healthy indoor plants and avoiding problems like root rot, overwatering, and underwatering requires proper watering practices. When watering indoor plants, ensure the soil is evenly hydrated, and the roots get enough water by thoroughly watering the plant until the water flows out of the pot without obstruction. Instead of watering plants on a set timetable, adjust your watering according to the demands of your plants and the surrounding environment. Regularly check the soil's moisture content and modify the watering frequency according to temperature, humidity, and light intensity. When the top inch of soil feels dry, indoor plants should generally be watered. Use enough water to thoroughly wet the root zone without flooding the soil.

In conclusion, watering equipment is a crucial part of indoor gardening since it gives gardeners the means and know-how to keep soil moisture levels at ideal levels and encourage robust plant development. Gardeners may ensure their indoor plants receive the moisture they require to thrive by choosing the appropriate tools and procedures for watering them and using the proper watering techniques. Practical indoor gardening requires careful selection and watering equipment, whether using sophisticated watering systems like drip irrigation and self-watering pots or more straightforward instruments like spray bottles and cans. Indoor gardeners may enjoy healthy, vibrant plants year-round, adding beauty and vibrancy to their interior spaces with the right tools and strategies for watering them.

Lightning Solutions (natural and artificial)

Artificial and natural lighting solutions play a critical role in indoor gardening, greatly impacting plants' growth, development, and general health. This section examines the significance of lighting solutions for indoor gardening and the advantages and drawbacks of both artificial and natural illumination.

Natural light is one of the most essential elements in indoor plant growth, which gives plants the energy they require for photosynthesis. The entire spectrum of wavelengths seen in sunlight is present, including visible light and wavelengths vital for plant growth and flowering, such as red and blue light. It's crucial to consider the natural light levels in your room when designing an indoor garden and to arrange plants so they get enough sunshine. Light-loving plants, like herbs, vegetables, and blooming species, thrive under south-facing windows because they receive the most sunlight during the day. While north-facing windows may offer restricted or indirect sunlight and are best suited for low-light plants like ferns, ivies, and snake plants, east and west-facing windows still receive enough sunlight.

While natural light is vital for indoor gardening, it may not always be available or consistent, especially in areas with limited access to sunlight or during the winter when daylight hours are shorter. In such cases, additional artificial lighting is necessary to provide plants with the light they need for healthy growth and development. Artificial grow lights, such as fluorescent, LED, and high-intensity discharge (HID) lights, are popular choices for indoor gardening due to their adaptability, energy efficiency, and ability to provide precise light spectra that meet plant requirements.

For indoor gardening, fluorescent lights are a widely accessible and reasonably priced choice that offers a well-balanced light spectrum that is ideal for various plants. Leafy greens, herbs, and seedlings grow exceptionally well in them because of their uniform light distribution and good coverage. LED grow lights have become increasingly popular because of their extended lifespan, energy efficiency, and adjustable light spectrum. Specific light wavelengths, such as red and blue light, are necessary for plant growth, flowering, and fruiting and can be produced by adjusting the LED lights. They work well with various indoor plants, including floral plants, fruit crops, succulents, and cacti.

More extensive indoor gardens or high-light plants benefit greatly from the intense light output produced by high-intensity discharge (HID) lights, which include metal halide (MH) and high-pressure sodium (HPS) lamps. MH lights are perfect for supporting robust, healthy foliage and vegetative growth since they emit a balanced spectrum of light comparable to natural sunlight. Red and orange wavelengths, abundant in the warm spectrum of light emitted by HPS lamps, are advantageous to plants in bloom or fruit. Although HID lights need extra components like ballasts and reflectors, they offer superior light penetration and intensity for indoor plants.

And suit the unique requirements of your plants, it's critical to consider aspects like light intensity, spectrum, duration, and coverage area when choosing artificial lighting for indoor gardening. Different plants require different amounts of light; some like direct, bright light, while others do better in less light. To guarantee the best possible light exposure and prevent problems like light stress or photobleaching, modify illumination intensity and duration by plant needs, development stage, and environmental factors. It would help if you also kept an eye on plant reactions.

To enhance artificial lighting and allow plants exposure to sunshine, combine natural light sources like windows, skylights, or light tunnels into your indoor garden design. Place plants close to windows or other natural light sources to encourage healthy growth and development to maximize their exposure to natural light. But be aware of possible problems like temperature swings, drafts, and direct sunlight, which can affect plant life and necessitate modifying plant placement and maintenance.

In summary, artificial and natural lighting systems are crucial components of indoor gardening since they significantly impact plants' growth, development, and general health. Indoor gardeners can ensure excellent indoor gardening results by evaluating natural light conditions, adding artificial grow lights as needed, and implementing appropriate lighting strategies and procedures to create ideal growing environments for their plants. Growing healthy indoor garden displays requires careful lighting solution selection and application, whether you're growing herbs on a kitchen windowsill or creating a tropical paradise in a sunroom. Indoor gardeners may enjoy healthy, vibrant plants year-round, adding beauty and greenery to their interior spaces with suitable lighting systems and maintenance.

Fertilizers and plant nutrients

Fertilizers and plant nutrients provide the vital components required for photosynthesis, root development, flowering, and fruiting, which are vital for the healthy growth and development of indoor plants. This section discusses the importance of fertilizers and plant nutrients in indoor gardening and provides information on their types, applications, functions, and best practices.

Fertilizers are concentrated supplies of vital nutrients that indoor conditions may not provide for plants but are necessary for growth and development. These nutrients include, among other things, micronutrients like iron (Fe), magnesium (Mg), and calcium (Ca) and macronutrients like nitrogen (N), phosphorous (P), and potassium (K). Every nutrient has a distinct purpose in the health and growth of plants; for example, potassium controls nutrient transport and water uptake, phosphorus encourages root development and blooming, and nitrogen supports leafy growth and chlorophyll production. Micronutrients play a crucial role in numerous physiological processes in plants and act as cofactors in enzyme activities.

Fertilizers come in various forms, such as liquid or soluble fertilizers, organic fertilizers, and synthetic or chemical fertilizers. Each type of fertilizer has unique advantages and considerations for indoor gardening. Artificial fertilizers are manufactured from inorganic materials, giving plants easy access to nutrients for quick uptake and usage. They are easy to use, inexpensive, and handy. Still, they could also contain high quantities of chemicals and salts, which can accumulate in the soil and lead to toxicity or nutrient imbalances over time.

Conversely, fish emulsion, compost, manure, and bone meal are natural sources of organic fertilizers, which offer plants a slow-release supply of nutrients. While they may take longer to decompose and release nutrients than synthetic fertilizers, they promote long-term soil health and fertility, improve soil structure, and increase microbial activity. For indoor plants, liquid or soluble fertilizers offer a quick and effective source of nutrients. They are designed as concentrated solutions that may be diluted with water and applied directly to plant roots or foliage. They can be tailored to match specific plant requirements or growth stages, making them perfect for use as foliar sprays or in hydroponic systems.

It's crucial to consider elements like plant kind, development stage, nutritional requirements, and soil conditions when choosing fertilizers for indoor gardening. To guarantee ideal nutrient uptake and plant performance, select fertilizers with balanced NPK ratios or formulas designed for particular plant demands, such as flowering or fruiting plants, to prevent overfertilization or nutrient burn, which can harm plant roots and leaves, adhere to the manufacturer's recommendations for treatment rates and frequency. Maintaining maximum plant health and vitality requires regular monitoring of plant growth and reaction to fertilization and adjusting feeding schedules or nutrient levels accordingly.

To boost plant nutrition and improve soil health, think about adding natural or handmade nutrient sources to your indoor gardening regimen in addition to synthetic or organic fertilizers. Excellent sources of organic matter and nutrients that help strengthen soil structure, boost microbial activity, and improve plant nutrient availability include compost, compost tea, worm castings, and seaweed extracts. In addition to offering a sustainable and eco-friendly substitute for traditional fertilizers, these natural amendments promote an all-encompassing strategy for indoor gardening that places a premium on soil health and ecosystem balance.

In summary, fertilizers and plant nutrients are vital parts of indoor gardening since they supply the ingredients required for plant growth, development, and general health. For the best nutrient uptake and plant performance, fertilizers should be carefully chosen and applied, whether synthetic, organic, liquid, soluble, or natural supplements. Indoor gardeners may produce vivid, healthy plant displays that flourish indoors by learning about the functions of various nutrients, choosing fertilizers according to plant demands, and incorporating natural nutrient sources into soil management procedures. An interior room may be made beautiful, joyful, and vibrant all year round with indoor plants that are well-managed and fertilized.

Miscellaneous tools (pruners, stakes, supports)

Inside gardeners' arsenals must include essential tools like pruners, stakes, and supports to help with indoor plant care and upkeep. This section explains the importance of this equipment for indoor gardening and discusses its many applications and advantages in detail.

Pruners allow gardeners to foster new growth, shape plants to desired sizes and forms, and trim away dead or diseased foliage—all crucial tasks for preserving the health and aesthetics of indoor plants. Pruning reduces the risk of pests and diseases by removing dead or damaged tissue, improving air circulation around plants, and encouraging branching and denser foliage growth. Pruners come in various varieties, such as bypass pruners, anvil pruners, and pruning shears, and each is appropriate for a specific type of plant and pruning activity. Anvil pruners are more suitable for cutting woody or dead material, whereas bypass pruners are perfect for making precise cuts on green stems and branches. Pruning shears are ideal for larger or more resilient stems and branches because they provide more cutting power and leverage. Maintaining healthy, vibrant, and aesthetically pleasing indoor plants requires routine pruning with clean, sharp pruners.

Stakes and supports are essential for giving indoor plants the structural stability and support they need to avoid drooping, sagging, or tumbling over. Provide vertical support and keep tall or top-heavy plants from bending or leaning under their weight; stakes are upright supports buried in the ground close to the base of the plants. Various materials, such as wood, bamboo, metal, and plastic, are available for stakes, and their height and thickness can be adjusted to accommodate a range of plant sizes and development patterns. To prevent breaking plant stems or roots, use robust, long-lasting, and smooth stakes on the outside. Climbing or vining plants grow more freely when supported by structures like trellises, cages, and hoops, which provide them something to cling to and climb on. While cages and hoops offer enclosed support for spreading or bushy plants, keeping them contained and erect, trellises are vertical structures with open frames that let plants weave and twine around them. In addition to improving plant growth and attractiveness, stakes and supports also assist in making the most of available space and producing eye-catching indoor garden displays.

Apart from stakes, supports, and pruners, a host of other auxiliary tools and equipment come in handy for indoor gardening projects. With the help of hand trowels and cultivators, gardeners may plant, transplant, and aerate the soil efficiently and successfully, even in small places. Gardeners can water plants softly and evenly without splashing or overwatering thanks to the exact control over water distribution that watering wands and spray bottles offer. Gardeners can modify watering and fertilizing schedules to suit plant requirements by using soil moisture meters and pH testers, which are crucial for tracking soil moisture content and acidity. To identify plants and record planting dates, varieties, and maintenance guidelines, plant labels and markers are helpful. Gardening gloves provide comfort and safety when performing duties in the garden by shielding hands from cuts, scratches, and dirt contact. Indoor gardeners may create stunning indoor garden displays that elevate the atmosphere of their living spaces and maintain healthy, happy plants by employing these various tools and accessories.

In summary, auxiliary tools like pruners, stakes, supports, and other attachments are essential to an indoor gardener's toolkit since they help with the upkeep, cultivation, and care of indoor plants. Gardeners can use pruners to reshape, trim, and revitalize plants, and stakes and supports offer stability and structural support to keep plants from growing lanky or toppling over. Apart from these fundamental instruments, various extras like handheld shovels, irrigation wands, soil analyzers, and plant labels enhance the effectiveness and efficiency of indoor gardening techniques. Indoor gardeners may guarantee their plants' health, vigor, and beauty and create eye-catching indoor garden displays that uplift and soothe their living areas by employing these instruments and accessories.

CHAPTER IV
Choosing the Right Plants

Low Lights vs. High-light plants

Several aspects must be considered while selecting indoor gardening plants, including the light each plant needs. Understanding these needs is crucial to the health and vitality of indoor plants since they have evolved to flourish in particular light circumstances. This section discusses the features of low-light highlight plants and provides tips for choosing the appropriate plants for various indoor settings.

Low-light plants can grow or endure low light levels; they usually get indirect or filtered sunlight during the day. By creating mechanisms to capture and use available light effectively, these plants have adapted to decreased light levels. To maximize light absorption, they frequently have more comprehensive, larger leaves or thinner foliage, and they could grow more slowly than plants that receive more light. Philodendrons, peace lilies, pothos, and snake plants are typical low-light plants. These plants thrive in spaces with little natural light, like north-facing windows or dimly lit interior rooms.

Conversely, "highlight plants" need robust and direct sunshine to flourish and realize their maximum growth potential. These plants need hours of direct sunlight daily to sustain healthy development and blooming because they have evolved to thrive in sunny, open habitats. Highlight plants may develop more vigorously and have smaller, more compact leaves or thicker foliage to tolerate strong sunshine than low-light plants. Succulents, cactus, herbs, and blooming plants, including citrus trees, roses, and orchids, are typical highlight plants. Indoor spaces with lots of natural light, such as south-facing windows or bright conservatories, are perfect for these plants.

It's critical to consider the available light conditions in your room when choosing plants for indoor gardening and to select plants that thrive there. Low-light plants thrive in areas of shade, interior places with little sunlight, and rooms with small or north-facing windows, among other conditions where natural light is scarce. These plants are less likely to suffer from problems like sunburn or leaf damage from prolonged exposure to high light since they may grow well in indirect or filtered sunshine. Since low-light plants usually need less upkeep and care than highlight plants, they are also an excellent choice for novice gardeners or those with little gardening expertise.

Conversely, highlight plants thrive in interior locations with lots of natural light, including rooms with large windows facing the south or west, sunny balconies, or outside gardens. For these plants to grow and flower typically, they need many hours of direct sunlight daily. Low light levels may make it difficult for them to survive. Highlight plants can make a statement or be a focal point in indoor garden displays because of their eye-catching leaves, vivid hues, or attractive blossoms. And avoid sunburn or leaf damage, it is crucial to keep an eye on light levels and offer sufficient shade from solid sunshine, particularly in the hottest parts of the summer.

When choosing plants for indoor gardening, it's crucial to consider the need for light and other elements like temperature, humidity, and available space. For certain plants to remain healthy and vibrant indoors, certain environmental conditions, such as high humidity or warm temperatures, may need to be satisfied. To make watering and maintenance chores more straightforward and guarantee that every plant gets the love and care it needs to flourish, consider grouping plants that require comparable care. Try combining different low-light and highlight plant combinations to make a unique, eye-catching indoor garden show that expresses your tastes and style.

When picking plants for indoor gardening, you should consider their light needs and choose species that will thrive in the light circumstances that your room provides. Highlight plants do best in bright, sunny conditions with plenty of access to direct sunshine, whereas low-light plants are best suited for interior spaces with little natural light, such as rooms with windows facing north. You may design a vibrant indoor garden exhibit that adds beauty and greenery to your house by knowing the distinctions between low-light and highlighted plants and evaluating the lighting in your area. Careful plant selection and maintenance depending on light requirements are crucial for excellent indoor gardening results, regardless of skill level. You may enjoy healthy, vibrant plants all year long that will provide delight and beauty to your interior spaces if you choose the correct plants and give them the necessary care.

Easy-care plants for beginners

Plants that require little maintenance are the best options for novices who want to begin indoor gardening successfully and confidently. Because of their resilience, flexibility, and low maintenance needs, these plants are ideal for anyone with limited time, expertise, or gardening abilities. This section examines several low-maintenance plants that are good for novices, emphasizing their traits, needs for upkeep, and advantages for interior spaces.

The snake plant, often called mother-in-law's tongue (Sansevieria trifasciata), is one of the most well-liked low-maintenance plants for novices. The beautiful foliage of snake plants, which have tall, upright leaves with variegated patterns in green and yellow hues, makes them so valuable. They can be used in nearly any interior setting because of their extraordinary resilience and ability to withstand a broad spectrum of light conditions—from dim to robust and indirect light. Snake plants are an excellent choice for busy or forgetful gardeners because they don't need much watering and can withstand drought. They are great options for offices, bedrooms, and other interior locations since they eliminate air pollutants like benzene and formaldehyde.

Another low-maintenance plant great for novices is the pothos (Epipremnum aureum), sometimes called golden pothos or devil's ivy. Heart-shaped leaves on pothos plants, which can be solid green, variegated, or marbled, are highly valued for their trailing vines and leaves. Because of their remarkable adaptability, they may flourish in various lighting environments, including dim and indirect light. Pothos plants are ideal for novices or people with busy schedules because they tolerate periods of drought and are tolerant of occasional neglect. They work wonders as air purifiers, assisting in removing dangerous pollutants and enhancing indoor air quality.

Another simple plant that is excellent for novices is the spider plant (Chlorophytum comosum). The characteristic features of spider plants are their gracefully hanging, spider-like plantlets and arching leaves on long, slender stems. Because of their remarkable adaptability, they may flourish in various lighting environments, from dim to high indirect light. Spider plants are appropriate for practically every interior situation since they can tolerate variations in humidity and a wide range of temperatures. They are ideal for inattentive or busy gardeners because they are low-maintenance and need occasional watering. In addition to being great air purifiers, spider plants also help to improve indoor air quality by eliminating dangerous pollutants.

Beginners will find the almost unbreakable Zamioculcas zamiifolia plant to be ideal. ZZ plants are highly valued for their elegant, glossy, dark green foliage and erect growth style, which elevate any interior area. They can withstand a broad spectrum of light conditions, from dim to intense, indirect light, and are resilient. ZZ plants are perfect for people with hectic schedules or little gardening knowledge because they tolerate drought and must be watered occasionally. They can survive times of low humidity and neglect, making them appropriate for any indoor setting. In addition to being great air purifiers, ZZ plants also help to enhance indoor air quality by eliminating pollutants like benzene, toluene, and xylene.

Spathiphyllum spp., or peace lilies, are another low-maintenance plant ideal for novices. Peace lilies are highly valued for their exquisite white blossoms and glossy, deep green foliage that lend sophistication and beauty to any interior setting. Because of their remarkable adaptability, they may flourish in various lighting environments, from dim to high indirect light. Peace lilies are perfect for people with hectic schedules or little gardening knowledge because they can tolerate periods of drought and variable humidity. They are ideal for inexperienced or forgetful gardeners because they are low-maintenance and need occasional watering. In addition to being great air purifiers, peace lilies also help to enhance indoor air quality by eliminating pollutants, including formaldehyde, benzene, and trichloroethylene.

In conclusion, novices who want to begin their indoor gardening journey with confidence and success should choose easy-care plants. These plants are ideal for anyone with limited time, expertise, or gardening abilities because of their resilience, flexibility, and low maintenance needs. There are several possibilities if you're searching for a low-maintenance plant for your living room, office, or bedroom. For year-round beauty and advantages, consider incorporating snake plants, pothos, spider plants, ZZ plants, peace lilies, or other low-maintenance plants into your indoor garden. Easy-care indoor plants may flourish and add delight and beauty to your home with the proper maintenance.

Specialty plants (herbs, vegetables, tropical, succulents)

Specialty plants are fascinating additions to indoor gardens since they come in a wide variety of species, each with its own special traits and needs. They provide unlimited opportunities for those who enjoy indoor gardening, ranging from water-storing succulents to lush tropicals, healthy veggies, and aromatic herbs. This section highlights the adaptability and beauty of herbs, vegetables, tropical plants, and succulents in indoor garden displays by examining their unique characteristics, maintenance requirements, and advantages.

Herbs are popular choices for indoor gardens because of their culinary use, medicinal qualities, and scented foliage. Common culinary herbs like parsley, thyme, basil, and rosemary are easy to cultivate indoors and add flavor to home-cooked meals. Herbs are suitable for sunny windowsills or well-lit kitchen counters since they like bright, indirect light and well-draining soil. Gardeners may enjoy fresh herbs all year round with regular trimming, which promotes bushy growth and extends the harvest season. Herbs used in cooking are not the only ones used medicinally. Herbs like mint, chamomile, and lavender are prized for their healing qualities and can be cultivated inside for their fragrant foliage and health advantages.

The vegetable garden is another type of specialty plant that may be cultivated inside with the proper maintenance. Certain vegetables grow well indoors and yield abundant fresh, nutrient-dense produce, but not all varieties are suitable for indoor growth. Because they take up little space and can be continually collected for salads and smoothies, leafy greens like lettuce, spinach, and kale are great options for indoor vegetable planting. It is also possible to grow small varieties of tomatoes, peppers, and cucumbers indoors in hanging baskets or containers, giving food access to fresh produce all year round. Provide enough light, water, and nutrients, and select vegetable kinds ideal for container gardening and small spaces if you want to produce veggies indoors.

With their vivid leaves and eye-catching blossoms, tropical plants lend an air of lushness and exotic beauty to indoor garden displays, taking gardeners to far-off places. With their diverse forms, sizes, and hues, tropical plants—from stately palms to vivid bromeliads and striking orchids—offer indoor gardener's countless opportunities. Tropical plants are perfect for bathrooms, kitchens, and other high-humidity spaces since they grow well in warm, humid settings with bright, indirect light. Well-draining soil and appropriate watering techniques encourage healthy root development and growth, while routine spraying helps regulate humidity levels and avoids leaf browning. Tropical plants add a little of paradise and a tranquil, tropical atmosphere to interior spaces with their gorgeous foliage and alluring blossoms.

Popular specialist plants with water-storing leaves, drought resistance, and distinctive textures are succulents. Succulents provide indoor gardeners with a wide variety of forms, sizes, and colors to choose from, including the recognizable rosettes of echeverias, the architectural forms of agaves, and the trailing vines of sedums. Succulents are perfect for sunny windowsills or well-lit interior spaces since they grow well in bright, indirect light and well-draining soil. They don't need to be watered frequently, so gardeners can enjoy low-maintenance landscaping without needing continual attention. Additionally, succulents are excellent choices for artistic container arrangements like terrariums, dish gardens, or vertical wall plantings, which give gardeners inventive methods to highlight these plants' unusual shapes and textures.

In conclusion, indoor gardening aficionados have countless options for adding beauty, flavor, and practicality to indoor areas through specialty plants, including succulents, tropical herbs, and veggies. Specialty plants provide something for every indoor gardener to appreciate, whether they create a tropical oasis in your living room, harvest fresh vegetables for home-cooked meals, or discover the fascinating world of succulents. Specialty plants can flourish indoors and add cheer, beauty, and energy to your house year-round with the proper maintenance and attention to their particular needs. Add herbs, vegetables, tropicals, succulents, or other specialist plants to your indoor garden to create a colorful and exciting indoor sanctuary that represents your interests and personal style.

CHAPTER V
Plant Care Basics

Watering schedules and techniques

The term "plant care basics" refers to various procedures necessary to keep indoor gardens flourishing and healthy, with watering schedules and methods being critical. This section explores the importance of watering schedules and methods for indoor gardening, providing helpful advice on setting up efficient watering schedules and using the proper watering methods to encourage the best possible health and growth for your plants.

Watering schedules are essential to indoor gardening because they determine how often and how much water plants receive, directly affecting their hydration and general health. Some basic rules are the watering schedule, even though it varies according to plant species, pot size, soil type, weather conditions, and seasonality. It's essential to evaluate plants frequently and modify the frequency and volume of watering according to their specific requirements and the current environmental circumstances rather than following a strict schedule. Because of this adaptability, indoor gardeners can adjust their watering techniques in response to changes in temperature, humidity, light intensity, and plant growth stages, all of which help to ensure that plants get the water they require to survive without running the risk of either overwatering or underwatering them.

It's crucial to consider the particular needs of every plant species and the distinctive features of their growth environment when creating a watering schedule. It's essential to adjust watering techniques to each plant's requirements because some plants require continuously moist soil while others do better in drier environments. To maintain ideal soil moisture levels and avoid water-related problems like root rot, fungal diseases, or dehydration, evaluating these factors and modifying watering practices as necessary is critical. Pot size, drainage characteristics, air circulation, and composition of the potting mix are some of the factors that affect watering frequency and volume.

Using the right strategies is just as important as creating a regular watering routine to ensure that plants get water properly and efficiently. Applying water directly to the soil surrounding a plant's base, as opposed to above, minimizes water splashing and lowers the possibility of fungal infections or leaf damage. Water can be applied softly and uniformly to the soil's surface using a watering can, hose attachment, or watering wand. That enables the water to seep deeply into the root zone and reach every area of the root system.

At every watering session, thoroughly wet the plants, letting extra water run off the bottom of the pot and seep deep into the root zone. Plants should not be left to sit in standing water since this can cause soggy soil, suffocate their roots, and ultimately harm their health. To avoid water accumulation and maintain appropriate drainage, dump any saucers or trays you may use to collect extra water as soon as you finish watering. Plants get water effectively and efficiently when appropriate watering procedures are used consistently, encouraging healthy root development, rapid growth, and overall plant vitality.

For plants or circumstances where precise soil moisture levels are preferred, such as plants with sensitive foliage, you may want to use bottom watering or sub-irrigation techniques. Plants are bottom-watered when placed in a tray or basin filled with water, and their roots are allowed to take up water via the holes in the bottom of the pot. This technique minimizes water waste and encourages effective water uptake by guaranteeing that water reaches the root zone. Sub-irrigation systems, like wicking systems or self-watering pots, suck water into the soil through capillary action to give plants' roots a steady source of moisture. These systems can assist in maintaining consistent soil moisture levels, which is especially beneficial for plants that demand a lot of water or that dry out rapidly. They are perfect for busy or forgetful gardeners.

For indoor plants, think about using mulching as an additional moisture-conserving approach in addition to appropriate watering techniques. Mulch, which can take the form of pebbles, gravel, or organic materials like bark chips or compost, helps control soil temperature, inhibit weed growth, and hold onto soil moisture, all of which improve plant growth conditions. To avoid moisture-related problems like fungal infections or stem rot, spread a layer of mulch around the base of your plants, leaving a tiny space between the mulch and the plant stem. Mulching, especially in dry conditions, can assist in eliminating the need for regular watering by reducing water evaporation from the soil surface.

In conclusion, watering schedules and practices are critical in plant health, growth, and overall garden performance in indoor gardening. They are fundamental components of plant care essentials. Indoor gardeners may encourage ideal plant health and development while avoiding water-related problems by creating a regular watering schedule, using appropriate watering procedures, and modifying tactics based on specific plant demands and ambient conditions. Appropriately applying appropriate watering strategies ensures that plants receive water effectively and efficiently. It enables healthy root development, rapid growth, and vivid foliage, whether employing conventional watering methods or cutting-edge irrigation systems. Indoor gardeners may create flourishing indoor garden displays and take advantage of the beauty and advantages of vibrant, healthy plants all year round by paying attention to watering schedules and practices.

Feeding and fertilizing

Nutrients are essential for plant growth and development, and indoor gardening relies heavily on feeding and fertilizing plants. This section examines the significance of feeding and fertilizing indoor gardens to encourage healthy, bright plants. It provides helpful advice on choosing suitable fertilizers, setting up feeding schedules, and applying the proper fertilization procedures.

Plants need various vital nutrients, including micronutrients like calcium, magnesium, and iron, and macronutrients like nitrogen, phosphorus, and potassium to sustain their growth and development. Even while some of these nutrients are found in soil naturally, indoor plants frequently need additional fertilizer to ensure they get enough. Fertilizers are designed to give plants the right amount of nutrients in the proper form, addressing nutrient deficiencies and encouraging strong growth and blooming.

It's crucial to pick fertilizers made especially for houseplants or indoor gardening when choosing supplies for indoor plants. Seek for well-balanced fertilizers containing vital micronutrients like calcium, magnesium, and iron and a balanced ratio of nitrogen, phosphorous, and potassium (N-P-K). Fertilizers designed for outdoor use or targeted plant species should not be used indoors because they may contain excess amounts of certain nutrients or chemicals that are harmful to indoor plants. Because of their natural origins and eco-friendliness, organic fertilizers like fish emulsion, compost, and manure are popular choices for indoor gardening. They gradually enhance the fertility and soil structure while giving plants a moderate, consistent supply of nutrients.

A feeding schedule must be established to guarantee that indoor plants regularly receive the nutrients they require throughout the growth season. Specific parameters are universally applicable, even though the frequency and volume of feeding depend on elements such as plant type, development stage, pot size, and environmental circumstances. When plants are actively producing new foliage, blooms, or fruit, which is usually the spring and summer, it is preferable to feed them indoors. During the fall and winter inactive or resting season, when plants require less nutrients and may be more vulnerable to nutritional imbalances or salt buildup, reduce or stop feeding.

Regularly check on plants and modify feeding plans according to their specific requirements and fertilization response. Leaf drop, stunted development, yellowing or browning of the leaves, and poor flowering or fruiting indicate an overabundance or shortage of nutrients. If a plant exhibits symptoms of a nutrient shortage, feed it more frequently or in larger quantities or use a fertilizer formulation that targets the particular nutrient shortage. On the other hand, if plants exhibit symptoms of nutrient overload or toxicity, cut back on feeding amount or frequency, water the soil to remove excess salts, and wait to fertilize until the plants have recovered.

It is essential to utilize appropriate fertilization methods to guarantee that indoor plants obtain nutrients effectively and efficiently. To prevent overfertilizing or nutritional imbalances, apply fertilizer according to the manufacturer's recommended dosage, application technique, and frequency. To reduce the possibility of scorching roots or creating a pile of fertilizer in the soil, dilute liquid fertilizers to half or quarter strength. Fertilizers should be applied directly to the soil surrounding the plant's base; do not apply fertilizer to the foliage, as this may burn or harm the leaves. After fertilizing, give plants enough water to prevent salt accumulation in the soil and ensure that nutrients are evenly dispersed throughout the root zone.

For a consistent, long-lasting source of nutrients for your indoor plants, consider including controlled-release or slow-release fertilizers. These fertilizers minimize the chance of overfertilizing or creating nutrient imbalances by gradually releasing nutrients over time, decreasing the need for repeated applications. Slow-release fertilizers can be mixed into potting mixtures or applied directly to the soil surface when planting. They come in various compositions, such as granules, pellets, or spikes. The polymer coating of controlled-release fertilizers progressively degrades in reaction to temperature and soil moisture, releasing nutrients into the soil as needed. By giving plants a steady supply of nutrients, these fertilizers encourage healthy growth and lower the possibility of nutrient excesses or deficits.

To sum up, fertilizer and feeding plants are crucial indoor gardening techniques that give them the nutrition they require to flourish and keep their best development and health. Indoor gardeners can encourage healthy, bright plants and take advantage of the beauty and advantages of indoor gardening all year round by choosing suitable fertilizers, setting up feeding schedules, and using the proper fertilizing practices. Indoor gardeners may produce thriving indoor garden displays and foster a stronger connection with nature by paying attention to nutritional requirements, feeding schedules, and fertilization procedures.

Pruning and trimming

Pruning and trimming techniques greatly aid in maintaining the health, form, and aesthetic appeal of indoor plants. This section examines the relevance of pruning and clipping in indoor gardening and provides helpful information on methods, best practices, and other useful information for growing vigorous, healthy plants.

Pruning removes some plant elements, including branches, stems, or leaves, to strengthen the structure, promote good growth, and improve the plant's overall appearance. Pruning helps lower the risk of pest infestations, fungus illnesses, and other health problems that might impair plant vitality by removing dead, damaged, or diseased leaves. Additionally, pruning encourages light and airflow through the canopy, lowering the possibility of moisture accumulation and enhancing the plant's general health. Furthermore, pruning enables indoor gardeners to train and shape plants to take on desired shapes or sizes, resulting in aesthetically pleasing arrangements and optimized use of available space.

Pruning indoor plants requires using clean, sharp instruments, such as bypass loppers, shears, or scissors, to make accurate cuts without harming the plant. Before pruning, ensure the plant is free of dead, diseased, or damaged leaves. It should also be free of any crossed or overloaded branches that could block light or ventilation. Remove any undesirable growth above a leaf node or lateral branch by making a clean, angled cut. Ensure the cut is made at a slight angle to encourage healing and minimize water buildup on the wound surface.

Pruning is an effective tool for indoor gardeners to educate plants to take on particular forms or sizes and remove dead or damaged leaves. Indoor gardeners can manage the overall size and shape of the plant, encourage bushier growth, and encourage branching by carefully cutting some branches or stems. It is constructive for making topiary or bonsai specimens with complex shapes or forms or for keeping compact, well-proportioned plants in small spaces indoors. Pruning plants regularly keeps them balanced and from growing lanky or overgrown, keeping them robust, healthy, and visually beautiful.

In contrast, trimming removes extra growth or foliage to maintain a neat, well-groomed appearance and encourage robust, healthy development. In contrast to pruning, which is primarily concerned with removing particular plant components, trimming is more about routine upkeep and styling to maintain plants at their best. Trimming can include taking out wasted blooms or fruit, tidying the plant's general appearance, or adjusting its size and form to fit in its allotted area.

Use clean, sharp tools, such as pruning shears or scissors, when trimming indoor plants to ensure the cuts are exact and do not injure the plant. To improve the plant's appearance, start by trimming off any dead or fading leaves, blooms, or fruits and any lanky or overgrown stems. Trim any long or unruly branches to maintain a tidy, compact shape. To enhance ventilation and light penetration inside the canopy, eliminate crossing or overloaded growth. Avoid stressing the plant by removing too many leaves at once, as this will prevent it from healing and growing again.

And maintain healthy development, enhance plant beauty, and stop the spread of pests and diseases, indoor gardening requires regular pruning and trimming. Indoor gardeners can guarantee that their plants stay healthy, bright, and aesthetically pleasing all year round by pruning out dead or damaged foliage, training and shaping plants to take on desired shapes or sizes, and keeping a neat, manicured appearance. Pruning and trimming can be rewarding and pleasurable components of indoor gardening with the right equipment, skills, and attention to detail. It can help gardeners create stunning, vibrant indoor displays and establish a stronger connection with their plants.

Repotting and transplanting

Repotting and transplanting are two important indoor gardening techniques that keep plants healthy, vibrant, and long-lived. This section explores the significance of repotting and transplanting, including information on the advantages of these procedures, the best techniques for carrying them out, and factors to consider for good plant maintenance.

Repotting is moving a plant from its current container to a bigger or different pot to make room for growth, add more soil, or treat situations where the roots are stuck together. Conversely, transplanting is transferring a plant from one place to another, from an indoor to an outdoor space, or from a nursery pot to a decorative container. Prevent root constriction, encourage healthy root development, and give plants enough room, nutrients, and growing conditions, these techniques are crucial.

Repotting offers the chance to replace and revitalize the growing medium, giving plants new nutrients and soil to aid their development—one of the main advantages of repotting is that potting soil can become compacted, nutrient-depleted, or contaminated with salts or pathogens over time, impairing root development and negatively impacting plant health. Gardeners may guarantee that plants have access to the nutrients and oxygen required to flourish by repotting them into new, well-draining soil. That will encourage strong root development and rapid growth.

By repotting, gardeners can evaluate the root system and address problems like root rot, circular roots, or root-bound conditions. Root-bound plants have outgrown their pots; their roots are now tightly packed and spiral around the sides or bottom of the container. That may limit the uptake of nutrients and water, impede root development, and cause stunted growth or decline. Gardeners can encourage healthy root extension and revitalize a plant by carefully loosening and untangling the roots and moving them into a larger pot with new soil. When repotting plants, it's critical to choose a container size and kind that accommodates root growth and facilitates optimal drainage. Choose a pot more extensive than the existing container to give the plant enough room to grow and spread out new roots. To stop water from collecting in the pot and creating root rot, ensure the pot's bottom has drainage holes. Please use premium potting soil designed for houseplants; ideally, it should drain well and be fortified with nutrients and organic matter to encourage healthy plant development.

Another crucial technique in indoor gardening is transplanting, which enables gardeners to modify plant positioning, enhance growth environments, and encourage general plant health and vigor. Transplanting plants offers a chance to change growing conditions, increase light exposure, and improve visual appeal, whether the plants are being moved from nursery pots to decorative containers or new locations within the house. Transplanting can also help reduce competition for resources among nearby plants, enhance air circulation, and limit overcrowding, leading to healthier growth and a lower chance of pest and disease issues.

When transplanting plants, it's essential to consider several factors, such as temperature, humidity, light exposure, and air movement, to guarantee proper setup and adaption. Select a spot that offers the right amount of light and growing environment for the type of plant, keeping in mind things like drafts, temperature swings, and direct sunlight. Give plants time to become used to their new surroundings by progressively increasing their exposure to light and adjusting to watering and humidity conditions.

To sum up, repotting and transplanting are critical techniques in indoor gardening that are necessary to preserve plants' longevity, health, and vitality. Gardeners can provide plants the nutrition, room, and growing conditions they require to flourish by repotting them into larger containers and fresh soil. It will encourage healthy root development and rapid growth. Transplanting enhances the aesthetics and health of indoor garden displays by enabling gardeners to modify plant location, improve growing conditions, and encourage general plant health and vitality. Repotting and transplanting can be incorporated into an indoor gardener's plant care regimen with suitable methods and considerations, guaranteeing the success and enjoyment of their indoor garden projects for years to come.

CHAPTER VI
Troubleshooting Common Issues

Identifying pests and diseases

One of the most important aspects of indoor gardening is troubleshooting common problems, such as spotting pests and illnesses so that gardeners can take quick action to keep plants healthy and vibrant. This section examines the significance of identifying and controlling pests and diseases in indoor plants, providing information on typical problems, identification techniques, and preventative and control measures.

Indoor plants are vulnerable to pests and illnesses that can harm their leaves, blooms, and roots and weaken their general health and vitality. Insects like aphids, mealybugs, spider mites, and scale insects are common pests. Fungus gnats and thrips are other common pests. These pests cause symptoms including yellowing or wilting leaves, stunted growth, deformed foliage, or apparent bugs on plant surfaces. They also feed on plant sap, weaken plant tissues, and spread illnesses. Furthermore, diseases that cause symptoms like leaf spots, mold growth, rotten roots, or withering foliage can spread quickly among indoor plants, including fungal, bacterial, and viral infections.

Early detection is key in managing pests and diseases. By regularly inspecting your plants, you can spot early warning signs of infestations or outbreaks, allowing you to take action before the situation worsens. Keep an eye out for any signs of mold, mildew, or rot on leaves, stems, or roots. Monitor plant health and growth patterns, noting any changes or abnormalities that may indicate underlying issues. Look for discolored or distorted foliage, webbing, stippling, or visible pests on plant surfaces. This proactive approach can help you prevent further damage to your plants.

It's critical to consider elements like plant species, growing environments, and environmental stressors that may exacerbate the issue while diagnosing pests and diseases. Knowing each plant species' unique needs and weaknesses is essential for accurate diagnosis and treatment, as certain plants are more vulnerable to particular pests or diseases than others. In addition, variables like temperature, humidity, light intensity, and airflow can affect the activity of pests and diseases. For this reason, it's critical to evaluate these variables and take care of any underlying concerns to avoid future problems.

Proper control measures must be implemented as soon as pests or illnesses are recognized. Mechanical techniques can assist in lowering insect populations and eliminating disease spores from plant surfaces. These techniques include hand-picking bugs, removing damaged plant sections, and gently watering plants. By making a habitat less inviting to pests and pathogens, cultural practices, including enhancing growth conditions, upholding good cleanliness, and avoiding overwatering or overcrowding, can also help reduce pest and disease issues.

Pest infestations and diseases can be managed chemically with insecticidal soaps, neem oil, horticultural oils, or botanical pesticides, in addition to mechanical and cultural control techniques. These treatments work by suffocating or repelling pests, obstructing the spread of disease, or altering their life cycle. When using chemical treatments, it is crucial to carefully read the label instructions and apply the product at the specified rates and times to reduce the danger of harming beneficial insects or phytotoxicity.

Retaining plant health and minimizing the need for intervention requires preventing pest and disease issues. Reducing the likelihood of insect infestations and disease outbreaks can be achieved by following proper plant hygiene practices, which include routinely cleaning plant containers, clearing away fallen leaves or other debris, and sanitizing instruments after each use. Furthermore, strengthening plants' natural defenses and lessening their vulnerability to pests and diseases can be achieved by routinely checking plants for indications of stress, nutritional shortages, or environmental imbalances and swiftly resolving any problems.

In conclusion, keeping indoor plants healthy, vibrant, and long-lasting requires solving typical problems like spotting pests and illnesses. Indoor gardeners may effectively manage pest and disease concerns and encourage healthy, vibrant plants by detecting pest infestations and disease outbreaks early, putting appropriate control measures in place, and exercising preventative tactics. With appropriate identification, timely response, and regular monitoring, indoor gardeners may minimize the danger of pest and disease issues while enjoying the beauty and advantages of indoor gardening.

Managing plant stress

Keeping plants healthy, vibrant, and resilient in difficult growth environments requires effective stress management, which is a crucial component of indoor gardening. This section examines the significance of stress management for plants, providing information on typical stressors, methods for detecting and reducing stress, and tactics for fostering resilience and overall health.

Numerous factors can affect indoor plants' growth, development, and general health. Everyday stressors include cultural practices like overwatering, underwatering, nutritional imbalances, root disturbance, and environmental elements like temperature swings, humidity levels, light intensity, and air movement. In addition, plants can experience stress from pests, illnesses, and physical harm, resulting in symptoms including wilting, yellowing leaves, stunted growth, or leaf loss. Identifying and treating plant stress as soon as possible is critical to stop additional harm and encourage recovery.

One primary method for controlling plant stress is improving growth circumstances to as near their natural state as feasible. To encourage healthy growth and development, provide plants with the right amount of light, temperature range, humidity, and air circulation. To guarantee each plant specie's utmost health and vitality, learn about its unique needs and modify growth circumstances accordingly. Additional lighting, humidifiers, fans, and temperature controls for indoor plants help create a more comfortable atmosphere that lowers stress and increases resilience.

It's crucial to routinely check plants for signs of stress to spot problems early and take appropriate action. In addition to symptoms of pests, diseases, or environmental damage, keep an eye out for symptoms like wilting, yellowing foliage, leaf loss, or stunted growth. Examine the growing environment and cultural norms to identify possible stressors, then modify them to reduce stress and encourage healing. Recently purchased plants, as well as those that have been repotted or transplanted, should be closely monitored since they might be more vulnerable to stress during acclimatization.

Careful watering techniques are needed to maintain ideal soil moisture levels and control plant stress. Avoid overwatering and underwatering, as these practices can stress plants and result in problems, including dehydration, nutrient imbalances, and root rot. When the top inch or two of soil seems dry, thoroughly water plants, letting extra water run off the bottom of the pot. Assess soil moisture levels with a moisture meter or your finger and modify watering frequency and volume according to plant requirements and surrounding circumstances.

Appropriate fertilization of plants can aid in stress management and encourage robust development. To prevent overfertilizing or creating nutritional imbalances, use a balanced fertilizer designed for indoor plants and adhere to suggested dosage and application requirements. Additional nutrients like organic amendments or micronutrients may be helpful to remedy specific deficits or improve general plant health. However, to avoid nutrient buildup or toxicity, it's crucial to check on plants and modify fertilization techniques as necessary periodically.

Regular pruning and grooming of plants can aid in stress management through increased airflow, decreased competition for resources, and removal of damaged or dead foliage. To promote new growth and preserve the shape and beauty of the plant, remove wasted blooms or leaves, prune away dead or broken branches, and clip back excessive growth. Remove any pests or sick plant material right away to stop the spread of illness and reduce stress on the plant.

When stress management strategies like gentle handling, appropriate transplanting, and acclimation are used, plants can experience less stress during handling or transportation. Repotting or transplanting plants should be done carefully to prevent transplant shock and disturbance of the roots. Give plants time to become used to their new surroundings by progressively increasing their exposure to light and adjusting to watering and humidity conditions. Giving indoor plants a steady, predictable growing environment can help lower stress and increase resilience.

In conclusion, sustaining indoor plants' resilience, vitality, and health under demanding growing circumstances requires effective plant stress management. Indoor gardeners may efficiently control stress and maintain healthy, vibrant plants by providing ideal growth conditions, checking on plants regularly, and using proper watering, feeding, trimming, and handling practices. By paying attention to plant requirements and ambient factors, indoor gardeners can reap the beauty and advantages of indoor gardening while lowering their risk of stress-related problems.

Dealing with common problems (yellow leaves, root rot, etc.)

A key component of practical indoor gardening is handling frequent difficulties like yellow leaves, root rot, and other problems. This section examines the significance of identifying and resolving these prevalent issues, providing information on their causes, techniques for identification, and management measures.

Indoor gardeners frequently deal with yellow leaves, which several things, such as nutrient shortages, overwatering, underwatering, insufficient light, or environmental stress, can bring on. Evaluating the growth environment and cultural practices is critical to identify the root reason for yellowing leaves. One typical cause of wet soil, root suffocation, and imbalanced nutrients is overwatering. On the other hand, foliage wilting, nutrient shortages, and dehydration can result from underwatering. Yellowing leaves can be avoided, and plant health can be increased by modifying irrigation techniques to maintain appropriate soil moisture levels and addressing nutritional deficiencies.

Another common issue that can damage indoor plants is root rot, especially those grown in containers with inadequate drainage or overwatered soil. Fungi that flourish in soggy soil conditions are the source of root rot, which results in the deterioration of root tissues and a subsequent reduction in plant health. Wilting foliage, yellowing leaves, stunted growth, and mushy or discolored roots are signs of root rot. To avoid root rot, ensure plants are cultivated in well-draining soil and pots with bottom drainage holes. If root rot is detected, remove problematic plant portions and repot the plant in new, well-draining soil to encourage healing. Refrain from overwatering and let excess water drain freely from the bottom of the pot to prevent saturated soil and root suffocation.

In addition, illnesses, nutritional deficits, pest infestations, and environmental stressors frequently encounter issues in indoor gardening. Aphids, mealybugs, spider mites, and scale insects are pests that can feed on plant sap, weaken plant tissues, and spread disease. It can result in symptoms like drooping or yellowing leaves, deformed foliage, or pests visible on plant surfaces. Diseases that affect indoor plants, like fungal, bacterial, or viral infections, can spread quickly and manifest as signs like leaf spots, mold growth, or decaying roots. Poor soil quality, incorrect fertilization, or insufficient light can all contribute to nutrient deficiencies, manifesting as symptoms like yellowing or discolored leaves, stunted growth, or poor flowering or fruiting.

It's critical to practice good plant care and implement suitable control methods as soon as possible to deal with frequent issues, including yellow leaves, root rot, and pest infestations. For early identification and action, it is essential to regularly monitor plants for indications of stress, insect infestations, or disease outbreaks. Regularly check plants for signs of disease, such as drooping or yellowing leaves, twisted growth, or apparent pests on plant surfaces, to detect potential stresses, make the required adjustments to support plant health and resilience, and evaluate growing conditions and cultural practices.

Integrated pest management (IPM) concepts, which stress preventing, monitoring, and controlling pests and diseases using cultural, mechanical, biological, and chemical means, are crucial to consider when tackling frequent issues with indoor plants. Cultural practices, including adequate watering, fertilization, trimming, and sanitation, can help stop insect infestations and disease outbreaks by making an environment less inviting to pests and pathogens. Mechanical techniques can assist in lowering insect populations and eliminating disease spores from plant surfaces. These techniques include hand-picking bugs, removing damaged plant sections, and gently watering plants. Predatory insects, helpful nematodes, and microbial agents are biological controls that can be utilized to organically regulate pest populations and reduce the need for chemical treatments. And minimize harm to beneficial insects and the environment, chemical treatments like horticultural oils, botanical pesticides, and insecticidal soaps should only be used as a last resort to control severe pest infestations or disease outbreaks. They should also be used sparingly and by label instructions.

In summary, managing typical issues like yellowing leaves, decaying roots, and vermin infestations is a critical component of indoor gardening and is necessary to preserve plants' resilience, health, and vitality. Indoor gardeners can efficiently manage common issues and encourage healthy, vibrant plants by practicing correct plant care, implementing appropriate control measures, and being alert for signs of illness or stress. Indoor gardeners can reap the beauty and advantages of indoor gardening while lowering the likelihood of typical problems and setbacks by paying attention to plant needs and environmental factors.

CHAPTER VII
Lighting for Indoor Plants

Understanding light requirements

Because lighting directly affects photosynthesis, which is necessary for plant health and vitality, indoor plant lighting plays a crucial role in their growth and development. This section explores the significance of comprehending the light needs of indoor plants, including solutions for supplying enough light and insights into the various characteristics of light and how they affect plant growth.

Photosynthesis, the process by which plants transform light energy into chemical energy to create glucose and oxygen, depends on light. This process requires energy, which light gives, making light an essential component of plant growth and development. However, not all light is created equal, and plants have certain needs regarding the type, quantity, duration, and spectrum makeup of light.

The color or wavelength of light is called quality, impacting how plants perceive and use light for photosynthesis. Blue and red light are the primary light spectrums that plants absorb; blue light stimulates vegetative development, while red light encourages flowering and fruiting. Plants need Green light in modest amounts for photosynthesis, albeit less easily absorbed than red or blue light. And choose suitable light sources and guarantee the best possible health and development for plants, it is crucial to comprehend light quality and how it affects plant growth.

Foot candles, or lux, are units of measurement used to describe the intensity, which is the brightness or amount of light available to plants. Different plants require different amounts of light; some thrive in low or indirect light, while others prefer robust and direct light. Evaluating light intensity is essential for determining whether a space is suitable for indoor plants and choosing the right light sources to satisfy their requirements.

Duration is the amount of time plants are exposed to light during the day, and it impacts how they develop and flower. For optimal growth, most indoor plants need 6 to 8 hours of sunlight daily; however, depending on the species and growth stage, some may need more or less. Encouraging plant health, minimizing stretching or legginess, and stimulating flowering and fruiting in flowering plants depend on providing an appropriate light period.

The distribution of wavelengths within the light spectrum is called spectral composition, impacting how plants perceive and react to light. A wide range of wavelengths are present in natural sunshine, including visible, ultraviolet, and infrared radiation. Selecting suitable light sources for indoor plants and supplying the required wavelengths for photosynthesis and other physiological processes require an understanding of the spectral composition of light.

There are various ways to provide light for indoor plants, such as grow lights, additional artificial lighting, and natural sunlight. Natural sunlight is the best light source for plants since it offers a wide range of wavelengths and different intensities throughout the day. But only some interior rooms get enough natural light, especially those with little window access or direct sunlight.

Indoor plants can benefit from increased artificial lighting, particularly in areas with low natural light levels. For indoor gardening, fluorescent, LED, and incandescent lighting are frequently utilized; each has benefits and drawbacks about price, energy efficiency, light output, and spectrum quality. Although economical and practical, fluorescent lights might need to give plants more light intensity. Although they can be more expensive initially, LED lights are adaptable and energy efficient. Although incandescent lights are less energy-efficient and generate much heat, they can augment light levels when combined with other light sources.

The ideal spectral composition and intensity for plant growth are provided by specialized grow lights, which are made especially for indoor gardening. Full-spectrum LED grow lights give a wide range of wavelengths appropriate for plants in all stages of growth, simulating natural sunshine. They are an excellent option for indoor gardening because they are durable, energy-efficient, and adaptable. They may, however, initially cost more than other kinds of illumination.

In conclusion, encouraging healthy development, flowering, and fruiting requires understanding indoor plants' light requirements. Indoor gardeners can choose suitable light sources and create the ideal environment for plant health and vitality by considering light quality, intensity, duration, and spectral composition. Enough light is essential for indoor plants to thrive, whether grown under specialized grow lamps, artificial lighting supplementation, or natural sunlight. Regardless of the amount of natural light available, indoor gardeners may take advantage of the beauty and advantages of indoor gardening all year round with the proper lighting.

Types of grow lights

Different grow lights are essential for indoor gardening because they provide artificial light sources that can replace or augment natural sunshine and meet the light needs of indoor plants. This section examines the several kinds of grow lights frequently used in indoor gardening, including information on their benefits, drawbacks, and factors to consider when choosing the best choice for a particular plant species and its growth environment.

For indoor horticulture, fluorescent lights are among the most often utilized grow lights because of their energy efficiency, affordability, and adaptability. The wide range of light wavelengths that these lights emit is ideal for plant growth, including the red and blue wavelengths needed for photosynthesis. Various varieties of fluorescent lights offer varying light intensity, efficiency, and lifespan. These include fluorescent tubes (T5, T8, T12) and compact fluorescent lamps (CFLs). Compact and easy to install into conventional light fixtures, CFLs are ideal for indoor gardening on a modest scale. Larger growing areas can benefit from fluorescent tubes' more even light dispersion. Fluorescent lights are affordable and work well with many different types of plants, but they might need more light to supply high-light plants or plants in advanced growth stages.

Grow lights with LEDs (Light Emitting Diodes) have become increasingly popular because of their extended lifespan, energy efficiency, and spectrum output customization. LED lighting is perfect for indoor gardening because it uses less energy and produces less heat than traditional lighting sources. These lights come in various designs, such as customizable LEDs with changeable spectral output to meet specific plant requirements and full-spectrum LEDs replicating natural sunlight. Because of its extreme versatility, LED grow lights may be adjusted to fulfill the light requirements of various plant species and growth stages. LED grow lights may cost more upfront than other varieties, but over time, they save money since they require less upkeep and energy.

Another choice frequently used in indoor gardening is high-intensity discharge (HID) grow lights, renowned for their excellent light output and efficiency. Metal halide

(MH) and high-pressure sodium (HPS) lights are examples of HID lights. These lights provide various spectrum outputs appropriate for varying phases of plant development. The blue-white spectrum emitted by metal halide lights is perfect for encouraging dense, compact plants and vegetative growth. The red-orange light spectrum emitted by high-pressure sodium lights is ideal for fruiting and flowering stages, encouraging vigorous fruit development and flowering. Although HID grow lights are solid and practical, they also generate a lot of heat; therefore, to keep plants from overheating, there must be enough ventilation and cooling.

Induction grow lights are a relatively new technology for indoor horticulture, providing long-lasting, low-heat output lighting options that use less energy. These lights have a longer lifespan and consume less energy than conventional lighting sources because they emit light using induction technology instead of electrodes or filaments. There are several spectrum outputs for induction grow lights, including full-spectrum models that are appropriate for every stage of plant development. Despite having a higher initial cost than other grow light varieties, induction lights save money over time by requiring less maintenance and energy.

The exact lighting needs of the plant species being grown, the size and arrangement of the growing space, and financial constraints all play a role in selecting the best grow lamp type. Full-spectrum LED grow lights provide adjustable spectral output and energy-efficient performance, making them a flexible choice for various plants and growth stages. While fluorescent lights are affordable for small-scale indoor gardening, they might need to offer more light intensity for plants in high light or advanced growth stages. Although HID grows lights are solid and practical, plants shouldn't overheat, so there needs to be enough ventilation and cooling. Although they could cost more upfront, induction grow lights provide long-lasting, energy-efficient lighting options with minimal heat output.

To sum up, different kinds of grow lights are essential for indoor gardening since they offer artificial light sources that can either replace or complement natural sunshine and suit the light needs of indoor plants. Choosing the best grow light source depends on several criteria, including the type of plant, its growth stage, its growing space, and budget. Grow lights can be fluorescent, LED, HID, or induction. Indoor gardeners may establish ideal growth conditions and encourage healthy, vibrant plants all year round with the correct kind of grow light.

Setting up and maintaining lighting systems

A vital component of indoor gardening is setting up and maintaining lighting systems necessary to provide enough light for plant growth and development. This section examines the significance of installing and maintaining lighting systems for indoor gardening and includes advice on optimizing light levels for strong, colorful plants.

And maintain plant health and best performance, several elements must be considered when setting up a lighting system for indoor gardening. The first thing to consider is choosing the right kind of grow light depending on the particular light needs of the plants being produced, the size and arrangement of the growing space, and financial considerations. Full-spectrum LED grow lights provide adjustable spectral output and energy-efficient performance, making them a flexible choice for various plants and growth stages. While fluorescent lights are affordable for small-scale indoor gardening, they might not offer enough light intensity for plants in high light or advanced growth stages. Although HID grows lights are solid and practical, plants shouldn't overheat, so there needs to be enough ventilation and cooling. Although they could cost more upfront, induction grow lights provide long-lasting, energy-efficient lighting options with minimal heat output.

The next step is to place and install the lighting fixtures to provide even light distribution and sufficient coverage of the growing area after choosing the correct type of grow light. Using adjustable hangers or chains to accommodate plant growth and upkeep, hang the lights at the proper height above the plants to provide the required light coverage and intensity. During the vegetative growth stage, place the lights closer to the plants to encourage compact, bushy growth; during the flowering and fruiting stages, move the lights higher to avoid light burn and encourage vigorous flowering and fruit development. To prevent overheating and guarantee safe operation, ensure the lighting fixtures are firmly fixed and well-ventilated.

Optimizing light levels and encouraging healthy plant development depend on lighting system maintenance. To avoid interfering with plant growth, periodically check the lighting fixtures, bulbs, and electrical components for indications of wear, damage, or failure. Replace any worn-out or defective parts right away. To maximize light output and efficiency, regularly clean the lighting fixtures and reflectors to eliminate dirt, dust, or debris. To ensure plants get enough light for healthy growth and development, use a light meter or spectral analyzer to track light levels and spectrum output. To account for variations in plant development stage, seasonal light levels, or environmental circumstances, modify lighting schedules and intensity as necessary.

Maintaining ideal operating temperatures and avoiding heat buildup in lighting systems require proper ventilation and cooling. To dissipate heat and prevent overheating, ensure the lighting fixtures have enough airflow and are adequately ventilated. They use exhaust fans or ventilation systems to keep the growth environment cool for the plants and remove hot air. For plants, avoid heat stress by using additional cooling techniques like fans, air conditioning, or evaporative cooling to control temperature and humidity levels. To maintain ideal growing conditions, periodically check the temperature and humidity levels and modify the ventilation and cooling systems.

When installing and maintaining lighting systems for indoor gardening, energy efficiency and sustainability must be considered in addition to routine upkeep and observation. To reduce energy use and running expenses, use energy-efficient lighting fixtures and bulbs with extended lifespans and high effectiveness ratings. To automate lighting schedules and maximize energy usage, use timers or programmable controllers to turn lights on and off at precise times to correspond with plant growth stages and light requirements. To lessen the environmental effect of indoor gardening operations, consider supplementing or replacing grid electricity with renewable energy sources like solar or wind power.

In summary, proper lighting system setup and upkeep are critical to supplying enough light for indoor plant growth and development. By choosing the right kind of grow light, setting and installing lighting fixtures correctly, and performing routine maintenance and monitoring, indoor gardeners may establish ideal growth conditions and encourage healthy, vibrant plants year-round. With careful care and attention to lighting systems, indoor gardeners can minimize energy usage and environmental effects while still enjoying the beauty and advantages of indoor gardening.

CHAPTER VIII
Temperature and Humidity Control

Ideal temperature ranges for different plants

Successful indoor gardening requires an understanding of the optimal temperature ranges for various plants, as temperature directly impacts plant growth, development, and general health. This section examines the significance of controlling temperature in indoor gardening, providing information on the ideal temperature ranges for different plant species and methods for preserving these ranges to support vibrant, healthy plants.

Due to the nature of their native environments, development patterns, and physiological functions, plants have specific temperature requirements. Certain plants require a particular temperature to flower or fruit, while others prefer milder temperatures. Certain plants even thrive in torrid, tropical climes. Selecting the suitable species for indoor culture and creating the ideal environment for their growth and development requires understanding the various plants' preferred temperatures.

Tropical plants, such as orchids, ferns, and tropical foliage plants, generally prefer warm temperatures ranging from 65°F to 85°F (18°C to 29°C). These plants do well in warm, damp conditions with constant temperatures all year round because they are used to humid, tropical regions. Enough warmth must be provided for tropical plants to thrive and avoid stress-related problems like wilting yellowing leaves or stunted growth.

Herbs, vegetables, and annual flowers are temperate plants that can withstand a more comprehensive range of temperatures and thrive in more varied environments.

The majority of temperate plants thrive in daytime temperatures between 60°F and 75°F (15°C and 24°C), with slightly lower nighttime temperatures. However, according to the species and growth stage of the plant, different temperatures may be needed. Extremes of heat or cold can stress plants and impair their growth and development. Thus, it's critical to maintain average temperatures for temperate plants.

Plants that thrive in lower temperatures, such as lettuce, spinach, and cole crops, like temperatures between 50°F and 70°F (10°C and 21°C). Because of their adaptation to cool, temperate regions, these plants do well in environments with moderate temperatures and lots of sunshine. For cool-season plants grown inside, maintaining ideal growing conditions and avoiding heat buildup requires sufficient ventilation and air circulation.

Temperature needs are specific for initiating and maintaining blooming and fruit development in flowering and fruiting plants. Colder temperatures are needed to develop flower buds in many flowering plants, including orchids, and then higher temperatures are required to encourage blossoming. Similarly, for fruit to set and ripen, fruiting plants like tomatoes and peppers need high daytime temperatures and slightly lower nighttime temperatures. Ensuring a plentiful harvest and encouraging flowering and fruiting in these plants requires maintaining the right temperature conditions.

Temperature changes must be carefully monitored and controlled in indoor gardening environments to maintain ideal temperatures. Various factors, including ambient temperature, humidity levels, air movement, and light intensity, can influence temperature levels in indoor growing environments. These factors can impact the health and performance of plants. Regularly checking temperature levels with a thermometer or digital temperature gauge will help spot possible problems and make the necessary corrections to keep plant growth circumstances at their ideal.

Several tactics may be used to control the temperature in indoor gardening spaces and provide the best possible growth conditions for plants. Dissipating heat and avoiding humidity buildup, especially in enclosed or cramped environments, requires proper ventilation and air circulation. Utilize air circulation systems, oscillating fans, or exhaust fans to increase airflow and keep the growth space at a constant temperature. Positioning plants away from heat sources like radiators, heaters, or direct sunshine in indoor growing environments can help reduce temperature changes and avoid overheating.

Maintaining ideal conditions throughout the year may necessitate additional heating or cooling techniques for temperature control in indoor gardening settings. Use heating wires, heat mats, or space heaters in the winter to add extra warmth and keep the temperature from dropping too much, which can damage plants. Use shade cloth, air conditioners, or evaporative coolers in hot weather to lower temperatures and shield plants from heat stress. Thermostats or automated climate control systems can control temperature and provide stable growing conditions for plants.

In conclusion, as temperature directly impacts plant growth, development, and general health, knowing the optimal temperature ranges for various plants is critical to practical indoor gardening. By choosing suitable plant species for indoor culture and creating the right conditions for their growth and development, indoor gardeners can establish year-round healthy and bright plants. With proper temperature monitoring and control, indoor gardeners may maximize plant performance and minimize stress-related problems while still enjoying the beauty and advantages of indoor gardening.

Humidity management techniques

Controlling humidity is essential to indoor gardening since it affects plants' health, growth, and general well-being. This section explores the significance of humidity management strategies for indoor gardening, providing information on how plants respond to different humidity levels, measure and regulate humidity, and maintain ideal humidity levels for solid and vibrant plants.

Humidity, defined as the amount of moisture in the air, is essential for controlling transpiration, nutrient uptake, and water balance in plants. The humidity needs of various plants vary according to their natural environments and evolutionary modifications. Desert plants, like cactus and succulents, are suited to low humidity levels, but tropical plants, like orchids and ferns, grow best in high-humidity settings. It's crucial to know which plants require varying humidity levels to provide the right growing conditions and guarantee the health and growth of your plants.

The initial stage of managing humidity in indoor gardening is measuring humidity levels. Relative humidity levels in the growth environment can be measured with hygrometers or humidity meters, giving essential details about the air's moisture content. 50% to 60% is the usual range of ideal humidity levels for indoor plants, while specific humidity needs may differ based on the plant type and growth stage. Regularly checking humidity levels can assist in spotting possible problems and implementing the necessary corrections to keep plant growth circumstances at their ideal.

Controlling humidity levels in indoor gardening spaces may need a combination of passive and active strategies to maintain ideal conditions. Passive humidity management strategies rely on natural processes to control humidity levels. These processes include clustering plants to create microclimates, employing humidity or pebble trays filled with water to boost ambient moisture levels, and proper watering techniques. Active humidity management strategies can be added to these easy-to-use and efficient approaches to maintain moderate humidity levels in indoor growing environments.

Active humidity management involves employing additional tools or technologies to control humidity levels in indoor growth conditions. In dry indoor areas, humidifiers can raise humidity levels, especially in the winter when heating systems tend to make indoor air drier. Various humidifiers, such as steam vaporizers, evaporative, and ultrasonic humidifiers, come with varying features, performance levels, and efficiency. Select a humidifier that fits the size of the growing space and has humidity levels that can be adjusted to suit the individual requirements of the plants.

In humid climates or during the summer, when indoor air is naturally more humid, dehumidifiers can lower the humidity levels in indoor growing settings. Dehumidifiers take out too much moisture from the air, which reduces the possibility of bug infestations, inhibits the growth of mold and mildew, and improves the growing conditions for plants. Several varieties of dehumidifiers come with varying features, capacities, and levels of efficiency. These include desiccant, hybrid, and refrigerant dehumidifiers. Select a dehumidifier that fits the size of the growing space and has humidity settings that can be adjusted to suit the individual requirements of the plants.

Adequate ventilation and air circulation, in addition to additional equipment, are crucial for humidity control in indoor gardening settings. Adequate circulation makes maintaining constant humidity levels, preventing stagnant air pockets, and distributing moisture uniformly throughout the growth area possible. Utilize air circulation systems, oscillating fans, or exhaust fans to increase airflow and give plants a more consistent growing environment. Place fans in strategic locations to guarantee adequate air circulation and reduce humidity stratification in the growth area.

To sum up, controlling humidity is a critical component of indoor gardening that is required to support solid and colorful plants. By learning about the humidity preferences of various plants, testing humidity levels frequently, and using the proper humidity management strategies, indoor gardeners may create ideal growing conditions and guarantee ideal plant health and growth. With correct humidity management, indoor gardeners may maximize plant performance, minimize stress-related problems, and enjoy the beauty and advantages of indoor gardening.

Using Humidifiers and dehumidifiers

Humidifiers and dehumidifiers are indispensable for maintaining ideal humidity levels in indoor gardening settings and guaranteeing healthy, vibrant plants all year round. This section examines the significance of dehumidifiers and humidifiers for indoor gardening, providing information on their advantages, uses, and factors to consider when choosing and using them.

Humidifiers are appliances that add moisture to the air to raise the humidity levels in interior areas. They are accommodating in arid locations or in winter when heating systems tend to make interior air drier. By releasing water vapor into the atmosphere, humidifiers raise humidity levels and improve plant growth conditions. There are various kinds of humidifiers, such as steam vaporizers, evaporative humidifiers, and ultrasonic humidifiers, that come with varying features, performance levels, and efficiency.

Evaporative humidifiers use a fan to distribute water vapor through a wet filter or wick, thereby increasing the relative humidity of the air. They are a well-liked option for indoor gardening because they are reasonably priced, energy-efficient, and require little maintenance. A fine mist of water vapor is created by ultrasonic vibrations and released into the air by ultrasonic humidifiers. They are ideal for various indoor gardening applications because they are energy-efficient, silent, and produce warm and chilly mist. To produce steam that is discharged into the air to raise humidity levels, steam vaporizers heat water using electricity. While they can quickly increase humidity levels, they may not be as energy efficient as other humidifiers.

On the other hand, dehumidifiers are appliances made to take out extra air moisture to lower humidity levels in interior spaces. They are accommodating in humid climates or during the summer when indoor air tends to be more humid. For dehumidifiers to function, moisture from the air must condense onto cold coils, where it must be gathered and drained off. Several varieties of dehumidifiers come with varying features, capacities, and levels of efficiency. These include desiccant, hybrid, and refrigerant dehumidifiers.

Refrigerant dehumidifiers use refrigeration coils to lower air temperature and condense moisture, which is subsequently gathered and removed. They are effective in eliminating surplus moisture from the atmosphere and preserving ideal humidity levels within enclosed areas. Desiccant dehumidifiers draw moisture from the air by absorbing it with desiccant materials like silica gel, which is then gathered and emptied. They are ideal for smaller indoor gardening spaces because they are quieter and use less energy than refrigerant dehumidifiers. Hybrid dehumidifiers effectively remove moisture from various indoor spaces by combining desiccant and refrigeration technology.

It's essential to consider the plants' unique humidity requirements while utilizing dehumidifiers and humidifiers for indoor gardening and to modify humidity levels appropriately. Most indoor plants enjoy 50% to 60% humidity, while specific humidity needs can differ based on the plant type and growth stage. To maintain ideal conditions for plant growth and development, check humidity levels frequently using a hygrometer or humidity meter and modify the humidifier's settings or dehumidifier as necessary.

Effective humidity control in indoor gardening also depends on the location of humidifiers and dehumidifiers. Place humidifiers close to plants or growth regions to provide proper moisture distribution and give plants a more pleasant atmosphere. Put dehumidifiers in places with excessive humidity or inadequate ventilation to remove extra moisture from the air and stop the growth of mold and mildew. Make sure dehumidifiers and humidifiers are the right size for the growing space and have humidity settings that can be adjusted to suit the individual requirements of the plants.

To sum up, to maintain ideal humidity levels in indoor gardening settings and guarantee healthy, vibrant plants all year round, it is imperative to use humidifiers and dehumidifiers. Indoor gardeners can cultivate plants and encourage growth and development by knowing the uses, advantages, and factors to consider when selecting humidifiers and dehumidifiers. Indoor gardeners may maximize plant performance, minimize stress-related problems, and enjoy the beauty and benefits of indoor gardening with correct humidity management.

CHAPTER IX
Air Circulation and Ventilation

Importance of air movement

Air movement is essential for the health, growth, and general well-being of plants in indoor gardening. This section examines the significance of air movement in indoor gardening, providing information on advantages, factors to consider when producing ideal airflow conditions, and specific methods such as using fans, air circulation devices, or natural ventilation for efficiently controlling air movement to promote plant growth and development.

Maintaining ideal growing conditions in indoor gardening settings requires proper air movement. Sufficient ventilation facilitates the even distribution of heat, moisture, and nutrients over the cultivating space, guaranteeing that plants obtain the essential elements for robust growth and maturation. Static air pockets can develop without adequate airflow, resulting in uneven temperature and humidity levels, a higher risk of disease and pest infestations, and decreased plant performance. By encouraging airflow, indoor gardeners can help their plants develop in more consistent environments, reducing problems caused by stress and enhancing plant health and vitality.

Temperature management is one of air movement's main advantages. In indoor growing conditions, airflow is essential for preventing temperature stratification and dissipating heat in enclosed or constricted spaces. Proper ventilation and air movement can help maintain the ideal temperature ranges for healthy growth and development. Furthermore, air movement lowers the threat of 'moisture-related problems' such as mold, mildew, or root rot, by preventing moisture buildup on plant surfaces.

Humidity control is an additional advantage of air movement. Proper ventilation prevents humidity stratification and lessens the chance of mold, mildew, and other moisture-related issues by assisting in even moisture dispersion throughout the growing area. The ideal humidity levels for plant growth and development can be maintained with proper ventilation and air movement, guaranteeing that plants get the moisture they require without experiencing excessive moisture buildup. Indoor gardeners may give their plants a more pleasant and favorable growing environment, lowering the possibility of stress-related problems and fostering optimal plant health by encouraging airflow.

In addition, air circulation is essential for the dispersion and consumption of nutrients. An appropriate airflow helps distribute nutrients evenly throughout the growing media, ensuring plants have access to the vital nutrients they need for healthy growth and development. To promote optimal plant nutrition and maximize plant performance, insufficient ventilation and air movement can aid in preventing nutrient imbalances and deficiencies. Indoor gardeners can establish a more effective nutrient delivery system for their plants and guarantee they get the nutrients they need for healthy growth and development by encouraging airflow.

Airflow not only helps regulate temperature, humidity, and nutrients, but it also fortifies plant stems and encourages robust development. Encouraging airflow causes plants to produce more 'ethylene ', a natural plant hormone that fortifies cell walls and encourages vigorous development. It is possible to prevent lanky growth and encourage compact, bushy plants with robust stems and robust root systems by ensuring adequate ventilation and air circulation. Indoor gardeners can facilitate appropriate plant design and reduce the likelihood of structural problems like bending, breaking, or toppling by encouraging airflow.

Careful planning and consideration of several parameters are necessary to provide the ideal airflow conditions for indoor gardening setups. Placing fans, vents, and air circulation equipment in strategic locations is crucial to guarantee enough airflow and distribution throughout the growing area. Place fans close to plant canopies to encourage mild air movement and avoid stagnant air pockets. They use oscillating fans or air circulation devices to prevent humidity stratification and establish a more consistent airflow pattern. When creating airflow systems for indoor gardening conditions, consider the dimensions and configuration of the growing space and the unique airflow needs of various plant species.

To sum up, airflow is a vital component of indoor gardening that keeps growing conditions ideal and encourages robust, healthy plants. Stronger plant stems and robust development are achieved through adequate ventilation and air circulation, which also helps control temperature, humidity, and nutritional levels. Indoor gardeners can reduce stress-related problems such as leaf wilting, yellowing, or premature dropping, increase plant health and vitality, and improve the growing environment for their plants by establishing ideal airflow conditions. Indoor gardeners can enjoy the beauty and advantages of gardening indoors year-round while maintaining the health and success of their plants with proper planning and consideration of ventilation requirements.

Setting up fans and ventilation systems

Assisting with airflow, controlling humidity and temperature, and establishing ideal growing conditions for plants are all made possible by adequately installing fans and ventilation systems. This section examines the significance of installing fans and ventilation systems for indoor gardening. It provides information on their functions, advantages, factors to consider when choosing the right tools, and methods for efficiently controlling airflow to promote plant growth and development.

Fans are essential to indoor horticulture because they encourage air movement and circulation throughout the growing space. Gentle air currents can be produced with oscillating or circulating fans to distribute air uniformly, avoid stagnant air pockets, and encourage gas exchange and photosynthesis. Place fans strategically to prevent damage or stress on plants to guarantee adequate airflow and distribution. Avoid placing fans directly in front of plants. In bigger indoor growing rooms, ceiling fans can also control humidity, temperature, and ventilation. By employing fans, indoor gardeners can foster a more pleasant and favorable growing environment for their plants, eliminating stress-related problems and encouraging healthy growth.

In indoor gardening settings, ventilation systems facilitate airflow and preserve ideal growing conditions. By removing damp, warm, and stale air from the growing area, proper ventilation encourages fresh air flow and keeps stagnant air pockets from accumulating. To promote airflow and keep plants in a suitable atmosphere, exhaust fans or ventilation systems can remove stagnant air from the growing space. Exhaust fans should be positioned carefully to guarantee enough ventilation and airflow throughout the ever-increasing space, avoiding places with weak circulation or stagnant air.

When setting up fans and ventilation systems in indoor gardening environments, consider the quantity and kinds of plants being grown, their airflow requirements, the size and structure of the growing area, and other aspects. Choose ventilation systems and fans that are big enough and built to last for the space needed for the ever-increasing area and the quantity of plants being grown. Consider using multiple fans or ventilation systems to ensure proper airflow and distribution across the growing area in larger or more intricate indoor gardening installations.

Fans and ventilation systems can help control temperature and humidity levels in indoor gardening settings and encourage airflow. Ventilation systems help create a more comfortable and conducive atmosphere for plants by eliminating excess heat and humidity from the growing space. That promotes healthy growth and minimizes stress-related disorders. To provide ideal growing conditions for plants all year round, regulate humidity, temperature, and airflow using exhaust fans or ventilation systems with programmable settings.

Proper maintenance and care are essential for the optimal operation and longevity of fans and ventilation systems. Fans, ventilation ducts, and filters should all be routinely cleaned and inspected to eliminate any dirt, dust, or debris that could obstruct airflow and lower efficiency. Replace worn or damaged parts immediately to maintain safe functioning and avoid airflow disturbances. Lubricate moving parts as necessary to keep them operating silently and smoothly to maintain ideal airflow and ventilation in the growing area, and check fans and ventilation systems frequently for indications of wear, malfunction, or performance problems. Then, make any required changes or repairs.

In summary, installing fans and ventilation systems is crucial for encouraging airflow, controlling humidity and temperature, and producing the ideal growing conditions for plants in indoor gardening settings. By carefully deploying fans and ventilation systems, indoor gardeners can create a more comfortable and favorable climate for plants, supporting healthy growth and eliminating stress-related concerns. By carefully choosing, installing, and maintaining fans and ventilation systems, indoor gardeners can enhance cultivation performance and improve airflow and ventilation in their growing environments.

Preventing mold and mildew

Preventing mold and mildew in indoor gardening is essential for crop protection, plant health maintenance, and a hygienic and secure growing environment. Because certain species of fungi, like mold and mildew, can grow in warm, humid areas with inadequate ventilation, indoor gardening settings are vulnerable to their development. This section examines the significance of avoiding mold and mildew in indoor gardening, providing information on the factors contributing to fungal growth, preventative measures, and methods for keeping a growing area free of mold.

Excessive moisture is one of the leading causes of mold and mildew in indoor gardening settings. High humidity, poor ventilation, overwatering, and poor drainage can all foster the growth of fungi, which gives mold and mildew the moisture and nutrients they need to increase. In indoor gardening, careful humidity control can prevent mold and mildew. They use fans, ventilation systems, and dehumidifiers to control humidity and encourage airflow. It will reduce moisture buildup and lower the chance of fungal growth. Using a hygrometer or humidity meter, check humidity levels frequently and adjust as needed to ensure ideal plant growing conditions and keep mold and mildew at bay.

For indoor gardening settings to be mold- and mildew-free, effective watering techniques are just as crucial as controlling humidity levels. Overwatering can result in soggy soil, inadequate drainage, and an abundance of moisture surrounding plant roots, all of which are favorable circumstances for the growth of fungi. To reduce the chance of mold and mildew, let the soil dry out in between waterings and refrain from overwatering plants. Reduce the risk of fungal infections by using potting mixes that drain effectively and containers with holes for drainage to encourage proper drainage and ventilation around plant roots.

Proper ventilation and air circulation are critical to preventing mold and mildew in indoor gardening settings. Pockets of high humidity and moisture from stagnant air facilitate fungal growth. To encourage airflow and circulation throughout the growing environment, avoid stagnant air pockets and lower the risk of mold and mildew, use fans, ventilation systems, and open windows or doors. Fans should be positioned carefully to guarantee adequate dispersion and airflow; they should be avoided in places with inadequate airflow or stagnant air, breeding grounds for mold and mildew.

When it comes to indoor gardening, keeping a hygienic and clean growth environment is crucial to avoiding mold and mildew. To prevent the growth of mold and mildew, it is essential to routinely clean and disinfect gardening tools, containers, and equipment. To lower the risk of fungal diseases and stop the growth of mold and mildew, remove fallen leaves, dead plant material, and organic debris as soon as possible. When managing mold and mildew outbreaks in indoor gardening situations, use organic fungicides or natural remedies like neem oil, hydrogen peroxide, or baking soda to stop the growth of these plant diseases.

Proper plant spacing and trimming can also help avoid the growth of mold and mildew in indoor gardening settings. Plants that are too close together may limit airflow and encourage moisture accumulation, which can foster the growth of fungi. Keep plants spaced apart enough to permit good ventilation and airflow, which lowers the possibility of mold and mildew. Regular pruning of plants minimizes the danger of fungal infections and encourages healthy growth by removing dead or damaged foliage, increasing airflow, and lowering humidity levels surrounding plant foliage.

In summary, controlling mold and mildew depends on keeping crops safe, preserving plant health, and providing a hygienic and secure growing environment. Indoor gardeners may easily prevent mold and mildew outbreaks and establish ideal plant growth conditions by controlling humidity levels, using suitable watering procedures, encouraging ventilation and airflow, maintaining cleanliness, and practicing good plant hygiene. Indoor gardeners may minimize the danger of fungal infections and promote healthy, bright plants while enjoying the beauty and advantages of indoor gardening with the proper preventive measures and procedures.

CHAPTER X
Growing Herbs Indoors

Best herbs for indoor gardening

Growing herbs indoors is an enjoyable and valuable way to keep your home smelling and tasting fresh all year. Herbs are adaptable plants that grow well indoors and offer gastronomic pleasures, health advantages, and visual appeal. This section looks at the best herbs to grow indoors, providing information on how to grow them, what to use in cooking, and growing suggestions.

Basil is a well-liked herb for indoor cultivation valued for its flavorful leaves and adaptability in cooking. This plant needs well-draining soil and steady hydration to grow successfully. It does best in warm, sunny weather. Many basil kinds, including Genovese, Thai, and lemon basil, are excellent choices for growing indoors since they have a variety of tastes and culinary uses. For a taste explosion, use fresh basil leaves to flavor soups, salads, pasta, sauces, and homemade pesto.

Another excellent herb for indoor cultivation is mint, which has a revitalizing scent and a pleasant taste. This herb grows best in indoor pots or containers since it likes shade and wet, well-draining soil. Spearmint, peppermint, and chocolate mint are popular varieties of mint grown indoors because of their cold, refreshing flavor, which goes well with a wide range of foods and drinks. Make your mint tea for a comforting and fragrant treat or use fresh leaves to flavor beverages and sweets.

Parsley is a valuable herb with bright green foliage and a spicy flavor. It is easy to cultivate indoors. This herb grows nicely on windowsills or in sunny interior spaces because it likes bright, indirect light and moist, well-draining soil.

Popular types of parsley for indoor cultivation are curly and flat leaf, which have different flavors and applications in cooking. Add fresh parsley leaves to homemade sauces and marinades for a burst of flavor, or use them as a garnish on salads, soups, stews, and pasta dishes.

A popular herb for indoor gardening, chives are praised for their delicate, grass-like foliage and mild onion flavor. This herb grows best indoors in pots or containers because it prefers bright, indirect light and wet, well-draining soil. Popular species for indoor production are garlic and common chives, which have beautiful cosmetic appeal and a variety of culinary purposes. Lift fresh chives to soups, sauces, stir-fries, baked potatoes, omelets, and salads to hint at onion flavor.

Rosemary is a potent herb that grows well indoors and is valued for its robust and pine-like flavor and aromatic foliage. This herb grows well indoors in sunny spots with sufficient ventilation because it likes bright, indirect light and well-draining soil with decent airflow. Many people choose to grow rosemary indoors. Varieties with unique flavors and culinary applications include Tuscan Blue, Arp, and Barbecue. Fresh rosemary sprigs give marinades, sauces, and infused oils a fragrant and aromatic touch. They can also flavor roasted meats, vegetables, bread, and savory foods.

Thyme is a multipurpose herb that grows well indoors and is valued for its earthy, lemony flavor and aromatic foliage. This herb grows best indoors in pots or containers because it prefers bright, indirect light and well-draining soil with sufficient airflow. Popular types of thyme for indoor production include English, lemon, and common thyme; these herbs have a variety of culinary applications and flavors. Fresh thyme leaves offer a delicious and aromatic touch to soups, stews, sauces, marinades, roasted meats, poultry, fish, and vegetables.

A popular herb for indoor planting because of its strong flavor and culinary adaptability is oregano. This herb grows best indoors in pots or containers because it likes bright, indirect light and well-draining soil with sufficient airflow. Popular kinds for growing indoors are Greek, Italian, and golden oregano; each has a unique flavor and application in cooking. Fresh oregano leaves can be used to marinades, salads, and infused oils for a savory and aromatic touch, or they can be used to flavor pizza, pasta dishes, tomato sauces, soups, and grilled meats.

Famous for its fresh, lemony flavor and vivid green leaves, cilantro is a popular herb for indoor planting. This herb is perfect for growing in pots or containers because it prefers bright, indirect light and wet, well-draining soil. In Mexican, Asian, and Middle Eastern cooking, cilantro is frequently used to give food a zesty, vibrant flavor. Fresh cilantro leaves offer fresh flavor to soups, stews, and sauces. They can also be used as a garnish for tacos, salsas, curries, salads, and rice dishes.

In summary, cultivating herbs indoors is a gratifying and helpful approach to savoring new tastes and scents all year. With various flavors, aromas, and culinary applications, basil, mint, parsley, chives, rosemary, thyme, oregano, and cilantro are excellent herbs for indoor planting. Indoor gardeners can cultivate these herbs indoors and enjoy their culinary delights all year long by providing the correct growing conditions, including enough light, moisture, and airflow. Indoor herb gardens can flourish and yield a steady supply of fresh herbs for cooking, garnishing, and experimenting with different recipes if given the proper care and attention.

Planting and care tips

Indoor plant planting and maintenance are both an art and a science, requiring patience, close attention to detail, and a thorough understanding of plant requirements. This section delves into the fundamental planting and maintenance guidelines for indoor gardening, providing an understanding of the major elements that affect the health, growth, and general well-being of plants.

The first step to successful indoor gardening is choosing the appropriate plants for your indoor space. When selecting plants for your indoor garden, consider elements like temperature, humidity, light levels, and available space. Select plants that are appropriate for your degree of gardening experience and the environment in your home. High-light plants like succulents, cacti, and herbs flourish in bright, sunny settings, while low-light plants like pothos, snake plants, and peace lilies are best suited for spaces with little natural light. Select plants that go well with your interior area's general style and decor and your personal aesthetic preferences.

For your indoor garden to succeed after you have chosen the right plants, you must use the proper planting procedures to ensure their establishment and growth. Please use premium potting soil designed primarily for indoor plants, as it offers the necessary nutrients, airflow, and drainage to promote vigorous root growth to avoid waterlogging and encourage proper airflow around plant roots; choose containers with sufficient drainage holes. Plant your houseplants at the appropriate depth, ensuring the dirt completely covers and supports the roots. To prevent overwatering and root rot, thoroughly water newly planted indoor plants to settle the soil and promote root development. Then, let the soil dry slightly between waterings.

One of the most important parts of caring for indoor plants is proper watering since both overwatering and underwatering can cause stress, withering, and plant death. Based on the unique requirements of your plants, create a regular watering routine that considers their size, type, development stage, and surroundings. Regularly check the soil's moisture content by sticking your finger to the first knuckle; if it feels dry, it needs watering. To prevent startling the roots of the plants, use room-temperature water and water thoroughly until any extra water drips out of the pot's bottom. As soon as possible, empty saucers or trays to stop water buildup and waterlogging.

Adequate lighting is as important for indoor plant health and growth as correct watering. Most indoor plants need bright, indirect light to flourish, while each type of plant may have different light needs. Ensure your indoor plants receive enough light throughout the day by placing them next to windows or in other naturally lit locations. Plants should be rotated frequently to encourage uniform development and stop them from bending or stretching toward the light. For example, plants in places with limited natural light—such as indoor rooms or windows facing north—may require additional lighting. If you want to illuminate your houseplants more effectively, implement cultivation lights or FSLs. Adapt the length and intensity of light exposure to your plants' growth stage and requirements.

Proper fertilization is another crucial component of caring for indoor plants, which supplies the necessary nutrients for muscular development and growth. Use a balanced liquid fertilizer designed primarily for indoor plants, diluting and applying it according to the manufacturer's instructions. During the growing season, which is usually from spring to fall, when plants are actively developing and creating new leaves, fertilize your indoor plants regularly. During the winter, when plant growth slows down and light levels are lower, reduce or completely stop fertilizing. Steer clear of overfertilizing, which can cause root damage, soil salinity buildup, and nutritional imbalances. For the best possible plant health and vitality, keep an eye on plant growth and alter fertilizer rates as necessary.

Ultimately, maintaining healthy indoor plants and averting outbreaks that could harm or ruin your garden depends on effective pest and disease control. Regularly check your indoor plants for symptoms of common plant diseases like powdery mildew, leaf spot, root rot, and indications of pests like aphids, spider mites, mealybugs, and scale insects. Use horticultural oils, neem oil, or organic insecticidal soaps to treat infestations immediately. Apply and dose these products according to the manufacturer's recommendations. To stop the spread of pests and illnesses, practice proper sanitation and hygiene by cleaning gardening tools and containers, removing contaminated plant debris, and not crowding plants.

In conclusion, creating the ideal growing conditions for plant health and vitality requires time, attention to detail, and a commitment to indoor plant care. You can build a flourishing indoor garden that adds beauty, freshness, and vitality to your home by choosing the ideal plants for your interior environment, utilizing proper planting techniques, providing adequate light, water, and nutrients, and practicing effective pest and disease management. When given the appropriate care and attention, indoor plants can bring years of happiness and satisfaction, improving your living area and helping you feel more connected to nature within your cozy home.

Harvesting and using fresh herbs

Fresh herb harvesting and use is a wonderful and fulfilling experience that lets home gardeners incorporate the bright flavors, scents, and health benefits of freshly harvested herbs into their everyday meals and cooking endeavors. This part delves into the art of harvesting and utilizing fresh herbs to optimize their flavor and nutritional content. It provides advice on how to harvest, store, and use herbs.

utilizing fresh herbs to optimize their flavor and nutritional content. It provides advice on how to harvest, store, and use herbs.

Harvesting herbs while they are at their freshest is crucial to thoroughly enjoying the flavor and fragrance of spices. Because most herbs' essential oils are most concentrated in the morning after the dew has dried but before the sun peaks, this is the optimum time to harvest them. To gather herbs, use sharp, clean scissors or pruning shears. Make clean cuts slightly above a leaf node to promote new growth. Steer clear of harvesting more than one-third of the plant's foliage at once to maintain growth and yield. Throughout the growing season, harvesting herbs frequently encourages bushier growth and keeps the plants from being lanky or woody.

The youngest, tenderest leaves from the outside of the plant should be harvested when picking leafy herbs like cilantro, parsley, and basil since they have the best flavor and scent. Harvest the top few inches of woody herbs, such as oregano, thyme, and rosemary, then trim them back to promote new growth. The best time to collect mint and lavender is when the blooms are just starting to open because this is when their essential oils are at their strongest. Harvest herbs right before using them to get the most flavor and freshness.

Herbs should be used as soon as they are gathered to maintain their flavor, aroma, and nutritional content. To remove dirt, debris, or insects, gently rinse the herbs under cold running water. Then, pat the herbs dry with a fresh kitchen towel or paper towel. Herbs should only be washed after use because too much moisture may speed up their deterioration. Herbs can be kept later in the refrigerator in a plastic bag or container lightly wrapped in a damp paper towel. As an alternative, herbs can be kept with the leaves above the waterline and the stems below in a glass of water, much like cut flowers. Change the water frequently to keep the water fresh and increase the plants' shelf life.

Cooking using fresh herbs enhances the taste, aroma, and depth of many foods, including salads, soups, meats, fish, and vegetables. Try various herb combos to find distinctive flavor profiles and improve your favorite dishes. Depending on the recipe and the user's desire, fresh herbs can be used whole, chopped, minced, or torn. Fresh herbs lose their power when cooked for an extended period, so add them at the end of the cooking process to maintain their delicate flavors and fragrances. Fresh herbs can also be utilized as garnishes to give completed dishes a burst of color and freshness.

Fresh herbs have many therapeutic and physiological benefits besides their culinary usage. Numerous herbs have high concentrations of essential oils, vitamins, minerals, and antioxidants that promote general health and well-being. For instance, parsley has a high vitamin C content and functions as a natural diuretic, while basil is well-known for its antibacterial and anti-inflammatory qualities. While rosemary enhances memory and cognitive function, mint is frequently used to ease nausea and digestive problems. Including fresh herbs can improve digestion, strengthen immunity, and advance general health and well-being.

A wide range of herbal treatments, teas, and infused oils for aromatherapy and natural skin care products can all be made with fresh herbs. For example, eucalyptus is frequently used in steam inhalations to reduce congestion and respiratory symptoms, while lavender can make soothing herbal teas and sachets. Use herbs like basil, thyme, or rosemary to infuse olive or coconut oil to create aromatic, fragrant oils that may be used for hair, skincare, and massage. Try various plant combinations and extraction techniques to make specialized herbal treatments that fit your unique requirements and tastes.

To sum up, home gardeners may enjoy the bright flavors, smells, and health benefits of freshly harvested herbs in their everyday lives and culinary creations by harvesting and using them, which is a beautiful and satisfying experience. You can maximize herbs' flavor, aroma, and nutritional value and improve your cooking, health, and well-being by adhering to the best methods for harvesting, preserving, and utilizing them. Herbs are a simple yet powerful method to add depth, flavor, and vigor to your food and everyday routine. You may grow herbs in a garden, on a windowsill, or indoors in pots.

CHAPTER XI
Indoor Vegetable Gardening

Choosing the right vegetables

Irrespective of the external climate or space constraints, indoor vegetable gardening provides a fulfilling and environmentally friendly means of growing fresh, wholesome produce all year round. The success and production of indoor vegetable farming greatly depend on the choice of vegetables. This section maximizes output and quality by discussing choosing the best vegetables for indoor growing by considering variables like space, light, temperature, and growth requirements.

When choosing which veggies to produce, the most important thing to remember is the area available for indoor vegetable gardening. Some veggies are better suited for more extensive indoor gardens or dedicated growing areas because they require a lot of space to grow and provide fruit, such as tomatoes, cucumbers, and peppers. Certain veggies, like lettuce, spinach, and herbs, grow well in smaller pots or vertical gardening systems, which makes them perfect for little indoor gardens. Examine all of the space in your house, including windowsills, counters, shelves, and vertical surfaces. Then, select veggies based on your space and the conditions under which they will flourish.

Another important consideration when selecting veggies for indoor growing is light. For most veggies to flourish and yield an abundant crop, they need strong, direct sunlight. Still, only some interior rooms have enough natural light to grow vegetables. If you don't get enough sunshine in your indoor space, plant low-light-tolerant vegetables or use artificial grow lights to supplement natural light. Herbs like parsley, cilantro, chives, and leafy greens like lettuce, spinach, and kale grow well indoors in low light and can tolerate little to no sunshine.

Considerations such as temperature and humidity are crucial when choosing veggies for indoor gardening. For optimum growth and fruit production, most vegetables require temperatures between 60°F to 75°F with moderate humidity levels. For best growth and yield, select veggies that are compatible with your indoor space's temperature and humidity levels. Root vegetables like radishes, carrots, beets, and leafy greens like lettuce, arugula, and Swiss chard grow well indoors in moderate temperatures, moderate temperatures, and manageable humidity levels.

The development requirements of various vegetables should be considered while choosing cultivars for indoor gardening. Certain crops, like tomatoes, cucumbers, and peppers, need a lot of area to develop and bear fruit since they are heavy feeders and must be fertilized often. Some, including microgreens, herbs, and leafy greens, don't need as many nutrients and can grow in smaller pots or hydroponic systems. Select veggies based on your level of gardening expertise and the soil, containers, fertilizers, and irrigation systems available for indoor planting.

Consider the time and effort needed for upkeep and care while selecting veggies for indoor planting. Certain vegetables, like tomatoes and peppers, must be pruned, trellised, and pest-managed regularly to maintain good growth and productivity. Some, like herbs and leafy greens, require less care and can flourish with little assistance. When selecting veggies, consider your gardening objectives and lifestyle, taking time, space, and resources for indoor gardening into account.

Finally, when choosing veggies for indoor cultivation, consider your tastes and culinary requirements. Select veggies that you want to eat and cook, that are easy to work within a range of recipes, and that are adaptable. To ensure a varied and well-rounded harvest during the growing season, consider planting various crops, such as leafy greens, root vegetables, herbs, and edible flowers. Try a variety of cultivars and kinds to find out which veggies grow best inside and fit your cooking tastes and taste preferences.

In summary, selecting the appropriate vegetables is essential for successful indoor gardening. Consider care needs, growth requirements, space, light, temperature, humidity, and gastronomic preferences. By choosing veggies that fit your indoor gardening space and your gardening objectives, you may maximize output and quality and have a plentiful crop of fresh, nutrient-dense produce all year long. The correct veggies may add happiness, fulfillment, and plenty to your house and table, whether you produce them inside vertical gardens, hydroponic systems, or containers.

Container gardening techniques

Container gardening techniques are a useful and adaptable solution for those who live in apartments or cities and have small or no outdoor gardens to grow plants in confined settings. This section examines a variety of container gardening practices, such as container selection, soil preparation, watering, fertilizing, and plant care, to assist gardeners in getting the most out of and enjoying container gardening.

For container gardening to be successful, selecting the appropriate containers is crucial. Several materials, sizes, forms, and styles are available for containers, each with pros and downsides. Pots made of plastic, ceramic, terracotta, and cloth are standard options for container gardening because they are long-lasting, visually appealing, and enable drainage. When choosing containers, consider the particular requirements of the plants you intend to grow in addition to size, weight, transportation, and drainage holes. Select pots that will fit your plants' root systems and offer enough room for development while maintaining stability, good drainage of water, and appropriate airflow.

That gives container plants a healthy growing environment and soil preparation is essential. Use premium potting soil specially blended for container gardening; it should be nutrient-rich, lightweight, and well-draining. Garden soil and topsoil should not be used in containers as they might become compacted, soggy, and devoid of vital nutrients. Potting soil should be poured into containers, leaving a few inches over the top for mulching and watering. For container plants, increase soil structure, water retention, and nutrient availability by adding organic matter such as compost, peat moss, or perlite. Throughout the growing season, incorporate slow-release or water-soluble fertilizers to supply vital nutrients for plant growth and development.

Providing adequate water to container plants is crucial since they are more prone to drying up than growing in the ground. Based on the unique requirements of your plants, create a regular watering routine that considers the kind, size, development stage, and surroundings. Ensure the entire root ball of the container plant is wet by thoroughly watering until any surplus water runs out of the pot's bottom. Regularly check the moisture content of the soil by sticking your finger up to the first knuckle; if the soil feels dry, it's time to water. Steer clear of overwatering, which can result in nutrient loss, fungal infections, and root rot. In container gardens, mulch the soil surface with organic materials like compost, straw, or shredded bark to help hold in moisture, keep weeds at bay, and control soil temperature.

Potting soil might eventually run out of nutrients. Therefore, fertilizing is crucial to giving container plants the necessary nourishment. Select fertilizers designed especially for container gardening, such as granular, liquid, or slow-releasing fertilizers, which offer a well-balanced combination of nutrients for the growth and development of plants. Fertilize container plants regularly during the growing season—from spring to fall when plants are actively developing and generating new foliage—by following the manufacturer's directions for application and dose. Steer clear of overfertilizing, which can cause root damage, soil salinity buildup, and nutritional imbalances. To maintain plants' best possible health and vitality in container gardens, keep an eye on plant growth and modify fertilizing rates as necessary.

Maintaining healthy container plants and boosting their growth and productivity require proper plant care. Container plants should be routinely inspected for indications of pests, illnesses, nutrient shortages, and environmental stress. Any problems should be promptly addressed. Examine plants for signs of common plant diseases like powdery mildew, leaf spot, root rot, and pests like aphids, spider mites, mealybugs, and scale insects. To stop pests and diseases from spreading to container gardens, treat infestations with horticultural oils, neem oil, or organic insecticidal soaps as soon as possible. You should also maintain high cleanliness and hygiene.

In conclusion, container gardening techniques provide a flexible and helpful approach to growing plants in small places, giving those who live in cities, apartments, and homes without extensive outdoor gardens the chance to grow herbs, beautiful plants, and fresh, nutrient-rich fruit. Gardeners may enhance their success and enjoyment of container gardening and create stunning, abundant gardens in any environment by adhering to best practices for container selection, soil preparation, watering, fertilizing, and plant care. Growing plants in pots and containers give you the delight of growing your food and flowers while fostering a connection with nature. You can grow plants on patios, balconies, windowsills, or indoors.

Pollination and harvesting

Two critical stages in a plant's life cycle are pollination and harvesting. These stages are necessary for the plant to reproduce and produce fruits, seeds, and eventually sustenance for humans and other animals. This section explores the mechanisms, relevance, and implications of pollination and harvesting for agriculture and ecosystems within the plant world.

The process of pollination, which results in fertilization and the formation of seeds, involves the movement of pollen from the male reproductive organs (anthers) to the female reproductive organs (stigma) of flowers. Although several plants can pollinate themselves, many depend on other natural pollinators, including wind, water, insects, birds, and other animals. Among the most frequent pollinators, bees, butterflies, moths, beetles, birds, and bats are essential to the global reproduction of flowering plants. Pollinators unintentionally gather and spread pollen from blossom to bloom while visiting them in quest of nectar, which promotes cross-pollination and genetic variation in plant populations.

Pollination is crucial for the health of ecosystems, the diversity of plant and animal species, and the growth of food crops. Its significance goes far beyond the ability of individual plants to reproduce. More than 85% of flowering plants on earth, including numerous crops including fruits, vegetables, nuts, and oilseeds, reproduce by pollination. Pollinators are necessary for these plants to produce fruits and seeds; otherwise, crop yields would drop, biodiversity would be lost, and ecosystems would deteriorate. Bees alone are thought to contribute billions of dollars to global agricultural production each year through their pollination activities, underscoring the economic importance of pollinators for human health and food security.

Gathering ripe fruits, vegetables, grains, or other plant products from cultivated crops for storage, processing, or consumption is known as harvesting. The timing of harvesting is essential since it affects the produced produce's nutritional value, flavor, and quality. Most fruits and vegetables are picked when they are at their ripest— when they have the best possible taste, color, texture, and sugar content. However, the ideal time to harvest a crop varies based on its type, growth circumstances, intended purpose, and consumer demand. Certain crops, like tomatoes and strawberries, are picked when fully ripe and fit for consumption, while other crops, like potatoes and carrots, are harvested before they reach their full maturity to maintain their delicacy and quality throughout storage.

Choosing ripe food, removing it from the plant, handling it carefully to avoid damage, and properly storing or processing it to preserve quality and freshness are some stages involved in harvesting. Berries, grapes, and leafy greens are fruits and vegetables typically harvested by hand because they need to be handled carefully or picked with care. For large-scale vegetable crops, grains, and cereals, mechanical harvesting techniques like combine harvesters are employed to speed up the process and lower labor expenses. The harvested product must be handled, sorted, and appropriately packaged to maintain its quality and shelf life, regardless of the harvesting technique.

Not only is harvesting essential to food production, but it also supports the livelihoods of millions who rely on agriculture for their income and survival globally. Harvest season is a time of celebration, get-togethers, and cultural customs in many rural communities. It symbolizes the end of months of toil and the wealth of nature. But harvesting can also present difficulties, like a lack of workforce, traffic jams, and volatile markets, especially in areas with poor infrastructure or market accessibility. Post-harvest handling, storage, and transportation infrastructure improvements in agricultural communities worldwide can help lower food loss and waste, improve food security, and sustain rural livelihoods.

The processes of pollination and harvesting are intricately linked to each other, supporting life on earth and the health of ecosystems and food systems around the globe. In contrast to harvesting, which gives us access to healthy, mouthwatering, and culturally significant foods from cultivated crops, pollination ensures the reproduction of flowering plants, genetic diversity, and the creation of fruits, seeds, and food crops. Through comprehending and valuing the significance of pollination and harvesting, we can collaborate to safeguard pollinators, promote sustainable farming practices, and guarantee food security for posterity. Let us acknowledge the critical functions that pollination and harvesting play in our lives and the earth's health, whether working in the fields, tending to our gardens, or having a meal with loved ones.

CHAPTER XII
Growing Exotic and Tropical Plants

Understanding exotic plant needs

Gardens can grow various plants from far-off places with eye-catching foliage, colorful blossoms, and exotic scents. Cultivating exotic and tropical plants is a singular and satisfying experience. But to cultivate exotic plants successfully, one must be aware of their particular requirements, which include those related to soil, water, humidity, light, and climate. To assist gardeners in successfully adding a hint of the tropics to their home gardens, this section examines the essential factors for cultivating exotic and tropical plants. It also sheds light on the nuances of these plants' upkeep and care.

Climate appropriateness is one of the most important things to consider while growing exotic and tropical plants. Many exotic plants are native to tropical or subtropical climates, distinguished by year-round warmth, high levels of humidity, and regular rainfall. As a result, it's crucial to choose plants that will thrive in the environment and growth circumstances in your area. Examine the natural surroundings of exotic plants to determine their preferred range of temperatures, relative humidity, and sunshine exposure. While certain tropical plants can grow well in warm, frost-free outdoor gardens, others may need shelter from the cold and would be better suited for indoor or greenhouse culture in colder areas.

Another crucial factor in cultivating tropical and exotic plants is their need for light. Most tropical plants have evolved to thrive in bright, indirect light environments where they are shaded by dappled trees or get filtered sunshine. Place exotic plants near windows or in robust and indirect light to replicate their native lighting conditions when growing them indoors. Tropical plants should not be placed in direct sunlight since this can result in withering, scorching of the leaves, and heat stress, especially during the hottest portion of the day. Indoor horticulture may require additional lighting, particularly in regions with little natural light or in the winter when daylight hours are reduced.

Exotic and tropical plants depend heavily on humidity levels for growth and development since many species need high humidity to survive. By regularly spraying plants, combining plants to create microclimates, or using humidifiers to raise the ambient humidity levels indoors, you can help them replicate the humid conditions of their natural habitats. Tropical plants should not be placed close to drafty windows, air conditioners, or heating vents since these might produce dry, arid conditions that harm the plants' health. Using a hygrometer, check humidity levels frequently and make necessary environmental adjustments to provide exotic plants with the best possible growing circumstances.

Growing exotic and tropical plants requires careful attention to the quality and content of the soil, as these plants need well-draining, nutrient-rich soil to flourish. Use a premium potting mix designed especially for tropical plants since it offers superior moisture retention, drainage, and aeration. Steer clear of utilizing garden or thick, compacted soils as they might get wet and cause root rot. Add organic matter to the soil, such as compost, peat moss, and perlite, to enhance the soil's structure, fertility, and moisture retention. Repot tropical plants frequently replenish the soil, give roots more room to spread out, and stop the gradual loss of nutrients.

Since exotic and tropical plants frequently have particular water needs based on their native habitat and development tendencies, watering is another essential part of caring for them. Most tropical plants require regularly moist soil but not soggy; in between waterings, the top few inches of soil should be allowed to dry out gradually. Give tropical plants plenty of water, ensuring that any extra runs off the bottom of the pot to avoid waterlogging and root rot. Steer clear of overwatering since this can result in root rot, fungal illnesses, and other problems with moisture. To avoid underwatering or overwatering, modify the watering frequency by climatic factors, including temperature, humidity, and exposure to sunlight. You should also routinely check the moisture content of the soil.

Finally, cultivating exotic and tropical plants presents a thrilling chance to infuse your home garden, interior area, or greenhouse with a hint of the tropics. Through a thorough grasp of the particular requirements of exotic plants, such as light, humidity, soil, and water, gardeners may establish ideal growing conditions and successfully cultivate these exquisite and distinctive examples. The secret to success is giving exotic plants the proper care and atmosphere to encourage their growth and well-being, whether you're cultivating them for their eye-catching foliage, brilliant blossoms, or exotic aromas. You can appreciate exotic and tropical plants' beauty and diversity in your garden or indoor haven with the proper care and cultivation methods.

Creating microclimates

In gardening and agriculture, creating microclimates is a valuable approach that enables producers to control climatic factors to create ideal growing conditions for plants in certain places or regions. Microclimates are small-scale climate zones impacted by topography, vegetation, water bodies, and human activity. They differ from the surrounding area regarding temperature, humidity, sunshine exposure, and other environmental elements. This section discusses building microclimates, their advantages and disadvantages, and workable methods for using microclimate management practices in landscapes, farms, and gardens.

One of the main advantages of establishing microclimates is the capacity to lengthen the growth season and increase the variety of plants that may be cultivated effectively in a particular location. Growers can cultivate heat- or cold-sensitive plants outside their native range by creating microclimates that resemble warmer or colder environments by manipulating environmental parameters like temperature and humidity. For instance, in colder climates, employing strategies like thermal mass, mulching, and row coverings can help shield plants from frost damage and prolong the growth season; in warmer climates, windbreaks, irrigation, and shading can reduce heat stress and produce cooler microclimates.

Microclimates can also maximize productivity, quality, and output by tailoring growth conditions for certain plant species or crops. Growers can construct microclimates perfect for the growth and development of specific plants by supplying customized environmental variables, such as solar exposure, soil moisture, and nutrient levels. For instance, maximizing solar absorption and heat retention by planting heat-loving crops like tomatoes, peppers, and eggplants in south-facing sites with total sun exposure will encourage vigorous growth and fruit output. Similarly, planting trees to filter sunlight or building shadow structures can produce the perfect growing environment for plants that like shade, such as ferns, leafy greens, and understory crops.

Additionally, microclimates can shield plants from harm and increase their general resistance by reducing environmental stresses like wind, rain, and extremely high or low temperatures. In exposed regions, windbreaks like fences, trellises, and hedgerows can assist in minimizing soil erosion and wind damage to plants by reducing wind speed and turbulence. Similarly, building retention ponds, swales, and rain gardens can aid in catching and storing rainfall, minimizing runoff and soil erosion during periods of high precipitation. Creating microclimates or sheltered places for plants can also help shield them from harsh weather conditions like frost pockets and pockets of cold air that can harm delicate plants due to frost.

Apart from their pragmatic advantages, establishing microclimates can augment the visual allure and biological diversity of gardens, landscapes, and outdoor areas. Growers may build diversified habitats that sustain a wide range of plant and animal species, fostering ecological balance and resilience by incorporating a variety of microclimates. To enhance habitat diversity and draw diverse pollinators, birds, and beneficial insects to the garden, grow a mix of sun- and shade-tolerant plants in different garden sections. Water features like ponds, streams, and wetlands can also provide visual appeal and biodiversity to the landscape by creating microclimates that support aquatic plants, amphibians, and other aquatic species.

Growing in microclimates has many advantages, but there are drawbacks that producers need to be aware of to be successful. Microclimate management involves meticulous planning, observation, and experimenting to find the best practices for particular plants, locations, and environmental circumstances. When creating strategies for managing microclimates, considerations must be made, including soil type, slope, drainage, and exposure to wind and sunlight. Furthermore, establishing microclimates could necessitate spending money on supplies, equipment, and upkeep (like erecting windbreaks, irrigation systems, or shade structures), raising prices, and complicating farming or gardening operations.

Moreover, maintaining microclimates necessitates constant observation and adjustment to accommodate seasonal variations, alterations in the surrounding environment, and changes in plant requirements. Growers must monitor plant performance, soil moisture content, pest and disease pressure, and other indicators to evaluate the success of microclimate management strategies and make necessary adjustments. For instance, to maintain ideal growing conditions and handle new obstacles in microclimate management, it might be required to modify irrigation schedules, prune trees, or construct more shade structures.

In summary, developing microclimates is an effective method for modifying environmental factors to produce the ideal growth environment for plants in particular locations or zones. Growers may prolong the growing season, improve growing conditions, and lessen ecological pressures in gardens, farms, and landscapes by comprehending the fundamentals of microclimate management and implementing proper techniques like thermal mass, mulching, shade, and windbreaks. Developing microclimates is a good investment for gardeners and farmers looking to maximize the productivity and sustainability of their operations due to the benefits it offers in terms of increased yield, quality, biodiversity, and resilience. However, there are obstacles and concerns involved. Growers may leverage the power of microclimates to create robust ecosystems that sustain various plants, fauna, and ecological processes by carefully planning, observing, and adapting.

Special care tips for tropical plants

Specific maintenance instructions are necessary for tropical plants to remain healthy, vibrant, and beautiful indoors and outdoors. Tropical plants are valued for their exotic foliage, vivid blooms, and unusual growth habits. They are native to warm, humid locations with rich biodiversity and luxuriant flora. However, there are difficulties with temperature, humidity, light, soil, and water requirements when growing tropical plants outside their natural habitat. To assist those who love gardening, landscaping, and interior plant life in creating verdant, tropical-themed outdoor spaces and indoor jungles, this section examines practical care advice and procedures for successfully maintaining tropical plants.

Setting up the ideal environmental conditions, including the proper temperature and humidity levels, is one of the most important things to consider when caring for tropical plants. Similar to the circumstances found in their natural environments, most tropical plants flourish at warm temperatures between 65°F and 85°F and high humidity levels between 50% and 80%. When cultivating tropical plants indoors, use air conditioning, heaters, humidifiers, and misting systems to maintain a steady temperature range and humidity level. To best grow and avoid sunburn, heat stress, and leaf damage, place tropical plants in areas with bright, indirect sunshine. Tropical plants shouldn't be placed next to heaters, air vents, or drafts, as they can cause temperature and humidity variations that harm the plants.

Because tropical plants frequently have unique requirements based on their original habitat and growth habits, light requirements are another crucial factor to consider while caring for them. Most tropical plants need bright, indirect sunshine or filtered sunlight beneath the tree canopy in their natural habitat. To guarantee that tropical plants receive enough sunshine for photosynthesis and growth when grown inside, situate them next to windows or in bright, indirect light-filled spaces. Additional illumination may be required for tropical plants growing in low light or in the winter when sunshine hours are reduced. To provide tropical plants with the ideal light spectrum, use full spectrum grow lights or fluorescent tubes. Vary the length and strength of light exposure according to the plant type, its growth stage, and its surroundings.

Another essential part of caring for tropical plants is watering them since their original habitat and growth patterns frequently dictate how much water they need. Most tropical plants require regularly moist soil but not soggy; in between waterings, the top few inches of soil should be allowed to dry out gradually. Give tropical plants plenty of water, ensuring that any extra runs off the bottom of the pot to avoid waterlogging and root rot. Water at room temperature to prevent shocking plant roots, and water early in the day to minimize the chance of fungal illnesses by allowing leaves to dry before dusk. To avoid underwatering or overwatering, modify the watering frequency by climatic factors, including temperature, humidity, and exposure to sunlight. You should also routinely check the moisture content of the soil.

Because they need well-draining, nutrient-rich soil to grow, tropical plants require careful attention to the quality and content of their soil. Use a premium potting mix designed especially for tropical plants since it offers superior moisture retention, drainage, and aeration. Steer clear of utilizing garden or thick, compacted soils as they might get wet and cause root rot. Add organic matter to the soil, such as compost, peat moss, and perlite, to enhance the soil's structure, fertility, and moisture retention. Repot tropical plants frequently replenish the soil, give roots more room to spread out, and stop the gradual loss of nutrients.

Because potting soil might eventually become exhausted, fertilization is crucial to providing tropical plants with the critical nutrients they need. Select fertilizers designed especially for tropical plants, like liquid, granular, or slow-releasing fertilizers. These types of fertilizers offer a well-balanced combination of nutrients necessary for the growth and development of plants. During the growing season—usually from spring to fall when plants are actively growing and producing new foliage—fertilize tropical plants regularly according to the manufacturer's application and dosage directions. Steer clear of overfertilizing, which can cause root damage, soil salinity buildup, and nutritional imbalances. For the best possible plant health and vitality, keep an eye on plant growth and alter fertilizer rates as necessary.

In conclusion, specific maintenance guidelines for tropical plants are critical to maintaining their vitality, health, and aesthetic appeal in indoor and outdoor settings. Tropical-inspired landscapes and indoor jungles that highlight the richness and beauty of tropical flora can be created by gardeners, landscapers, and lovers of indoor plants by setting up the proper climatic variables, such as temperature, humidity, light, soil, and water requirements. Tropical plants may flourish and add a hint of the tropics to any environment with proper maintenance and attention to detail. Their exotic foliage, colorful blossoms, and unusual growth patterns can enhance our lives. These maintenance suggestions can help you succeed and create a gorgeous tropical hideaway to enjoy all year round, whether you're growing tropical plants indoors, designing an outdoor tropical garden, or adding tropical elements to your landscape design.

CHAPTER XIII
Hydroponic and Aquaponic Systems

Basics of hydroponics

Growing plants without soil by using nutrient-rich water solutions is known as hydroponics. It's a cutting-edge and well-liked agricultural technique that has many advantages over conventional soil-based farming. Learning about the fundamentals of hydroponics includes investigating its various systems, benefits, and drawbacks. By exploring these facets, this part thoroughly introduces hydroponics and highlights its importance in contemporary agriculture.

The fundamental idea behind hydroponics is to provide plants with all the nutrients they require directly through water, doing away with the need for soil. With this technique, the growth environment, including fertilizer concentrations, pH levels, and water quality, may be precisely controlled. Hydroponics lowers the risk of soil-borne illnesses and pests by doing away with soil, which in conventional farming can substantially influence plant health and productivity. Furthermore, hydroponics' controlled atmosphere makes it possible to cultivate year-round, regardless of weather or seasonal variations, improving food availability and security.

Numerous hydroponic systems have been created to accommodate various plant species, production levels, and resource accessibility. Aeroponics, drip systems, deep water culture (DWC), and nutrient film technique (NFT) are a few of the most popular systems. Due to their distinct features and uses, each system can be used with various crops and growing environments.

The plant roots, maintained in a thin film or shallow channel, are continuously covered with a nutritional solution using the nutrient film method (NFT). This technique works exceptionally well for leafy greens and herbs because it constantly supplies the roots with nutrients and oxygen. Because of the nutrient film's shallow depth, roots are guaranteed enough oxygen, which keeps them from waterlogging and encourages vigorous growth. However, NFT systems need careful monitoring and upkeep to avoid nutritional imbalances and ensure steady flow rates.

Another well-liked hydroponic technique is deep water culture (DWC), in which plant roots are suspended in a nutrient-rich water solution. An air pump ensures the water is oxygenated enough for roots to breathe. DWC systems are perfect for novices and small-scale farmers because they are comparatively easy to set up and maintain. They work incredibly well for producing water-loving, quickly growing plants like spinach and lettuce. That avoid root rot and other problems, DWC systems must be closely monitored and susceptible to temperature changes.

A more sophisticated hydroponic system called aeroponics includes hanging plant roots in the air and regularly spraying them with a nutritional solution. This technique offers the ideal oxygen, water, and nutrients ratio, encouraging quick growth and large yields. Environmental sustainability is a feature of aeroponics systems since they are highly effective and require less water and nutrients than other hydroponic techniques. However, it might be challenging for inexperienced growers to maintain and precisely control the amounts of humidity, fertilizer concentrations, and misting intervals.

Using a series of tubes and emitters, drip systems—also called drip irrigation or fertigation systems—involve giving nutrient solutions straight to the root of every plant.

This approach is easily scalable for both small and extensive operations, and it provides exact control over the distribution of nutrients. Since they are so adaptable, vegetables, fruits, and flowers can all be grown with drip systems. They need routine maintenance to avoid clogging and guarantee even fertilizer distribution.

One of hydroponics' main advantages is its capacity to attain greater yields and quicker development rates compared to conventional soil-based agriculture. Because nutrients are delivered to plant roots directly and effectively, minimizing energy expenditure on root development and maximizing growth above ground. Furthermore, the hydroponic system's regulated climate lessens the need for chemical herbicides and pesticides, producing cleaner, healthier produce.

Due to the closed-loop systems utilized in many hydroponic setups, which recycle and reuse water, hydroponics also provides significant water savings. This is especially crucial in areas experiencing drought or a lack of water. Moreover, hydroponics may be employed in cities, using rooftops, vertical spaces, and vacant buildings to grow fresh, locally sourced food and lessen the carbon footprint of transporting it over great distances.

Hydroponics has many advantages, but growers must also overcome several difficulties to succeed. Hydroponic systems can have expensive initial startup expenses since they need to invest in technology, infrastructure, and equipment. Furthermore, compared to conventional farming, hydroponics demands excellent technical know-how and proficiency since producers need to monitor and regulate several variables, including nutrient concentrations, pH levels, and water quality. Nutrient imbalances, root infections, and system malfunctions can all be avoided with routine maintenance and observation.

Another factor to consider is energy consumption, especially for indoor hydroponic systems that depend on artificial lighting. Although the development of energy-efficient LED lighting has eased some of these worries, farmers still need to consider the energy needs of pumps, air systems, and climate control equipment. Hydroponic businesses must balance energy use with environmental methods to be viable over the long run.

To sum up, hydroponics is a cutting-edge and promising farming method with several advantages, such as increased yields, quicker growth rates, less water usage, and the capacity to cultivate food in metropolitan areas. Growers may take advantage of the promise of hydroponics to produce abundant, healthy, and sustainable crops by learning the techniques' fundamentals and the available systems. Even though hydroponics has drawbacks in terms of cost, technical expertise, and energy usage, research and development are constantly improving the effectiveness and accessibility of this innovative farming method and ensuring food security and sustainability for future generations; hydroponics will become more and more crucial as the world's population grows and environmental constraints rise.

Setting up a hydroponic garden

A hydroponic garden requires careful planning and execution of multiple essential procedures to guarantee that plants get the light, water, and nutrients they need to flourish without soil. Growing plants in a nutrient-rich water solution, or hydroponics, can yield larger yields than conventional soil-based gardening and allows for more economical use of resources. The crucial actions and factors for establishing a productive hydroponic garden are described in this part. These include picking a good site, deciding on a hydroponic system, getting the growing media ready, and caring for the garden.

The first crucial step in creating a hydroponic garden is selecting a suitable location. Water and electricity must be available sufficiently in the area for the hydroponic system to function. Ideal locations include inside areas like garages, basements, or grow rooms since they provide more control over environmental factors like light, humidity, and temperature. If the garden is to be set up outside, the space must have access to artificial lighting or enough sunshine. The area must also be clean and clear of any pollutants that can endanger the plants.

The next stage is to choose the right hydroponic system, which is determined by the kind of plants you want to grow, the amount of space you have available, and your financial situation. Growers use a variety of hydroponic systems, each with pros and cons of its own. For example, the plant roots in the nutritional film technique (NFT) system are maintained in a thin film or shallow channel, and a continuous flow of nutrient solution is applied over them. It's the best system for herbs and leafy greens. The deep water culture (DWC) method is appropriate for quickly developing, water-loving plants like lettuce and spinach because it suspends plant roots in a nutrient-rich water solution. Aeroponics is very effective and uses less water because plant roots are regularly misted with a nutritional solution. However, it does require careful control and upkeep. Through a network of tubes and emitters, the drip system directly provides nutrient solutions to the base of every plant, making it adaptable and expandable for various crops.

The next step is to prepare the growing media after selecting a hydroponic system. Soil is not used in hydroponic growing, unlike traditional gardening. Instead, using inert growing material provides aeration and support for the plant roots. Clay pellets, perlite, vermiculite, rock wool, and coconut coir are examples of standard growing media. Distinctive characteristics of every medium impact water retention, drainage, and aeration. For instance, rock wool works well in many hydroponic systems because it offers good aeration and water retention. Aeration and water retention are provided by coconut coir, a sustainable product from coconut husks. The lightweight, porous elements perlite and vermiculite enhance drainage and aeration when used with other media. Hydroton, another name for clay pellets, is reusable and offers superior aeration and drainage.

The chosen equipment and growing media must be installed in the hydroponic garden. It entails assembling the system's parts, including growing containers, tubing, pumps, and reservoirs. Ensuring the security of all connections and watertightness of the system is crucial to prevent leaks and preserve a steady growing environment. The preparation of the nutrient solution, which gives the plants vital minerals and nutrients, must consider the particular needs of the plants that have been selected. The solution—usually generated by diluting concentrated nutrient formulations in water—must be continuously checked and modified for pH and nutrient concentration to maintain ideal plant growth.

Another important consideration when building a hydroponic garden is lighting, particularly for indoor installations. Photosynthesis in plants depends on light, and the amount, kind, and length of light exposure directly affects the growth and development of plants. Although natural sunlight is preferred, artificial lighting can be used in addition to or instead of it. Examples of artificial lighting include fluorescent, LED, and high-intensity discharge (HID) lamps. LED lights are well-liked for hydroponic applications because of their extended lifespan, broad-spectrum light output, and energy efficiency. A suitable distance between the lights and the plants is necessary to avoid overheating and guarantee uniform light dispersion. A timer can also be used to automate the light cycle, which gives most plants 16–18 hours of light per day on average.

A hydroponic garden needs to be regularly monitored and adjusted to maintain ideal growing conditions. Implicates measuring the electrical conductivity (EC) and pH of the nutrient solution show the amount of dissolved nutrients present. Maintaining the pH level within the ideal range for the particular plants—typically between 5.5 and 6.5—will guarantee nutrient availability and uptake. Additionally, the nutrient solution must be changed regularly to avoid salt accumulation and nutrient imbalances. To prevent heat stress and encourage healthy growth, keeping an eye on the temperature and humidity conditions is critical. Keep the right conditions; indoor gardens could need extra tools like fans, heaters, or humidifiers.

Managing pests and diseases is equally crucial for hydroponic gardening. While soil-borne pests and diseases are less familiar with hydroponic gardening, airborne infections, and insect infestations can still affect plants. Plant health can be preserved by regularly checking plants for indications of pests or diseases and by using integrated pest management (IPM) techniques. That could entail employing cultural techniques like crop rotation, utilizing biological controls like beneficial insects, and administering chemical or organic treatments as required.

In conclusion, meticulous preparation and attention to detail are necessary to build up a hydroponic garden to provide the best possible growing conditions for plants. Growers can accomplish successful hydroponic cultivation by picking a good location, choosing a suitable hydroponic system, preparing the growing medium, and ensuring the lighting and maintenance are done correctly. This gardening technique benefits both hobbyists and commercial growers because of its many benefits, including adequate resource use, increased yields, and the capacity to grow plants in a controlled environment. Hydroponic gardening may be a fulfilling and sustainable method to grow fresh, nutritious plants all year round, provided you have the necessary information and tools.

Introduction to aquaponics

Aquaponics, a sustainable farming technique that combines hydroponics—growing plants without soil—and aquaculture—raising fish—offers a creative and effective way to produce food. By utilizing the inherent interactions between aquatic plants and animals, this integrated system creates a self-sustaining cycle that is advantageous to both. Gardeners and farmers may maximize the potential of aquaponics to provide fresh, healthful food with minimal environmental effects by learning about its components and guiding principles.

Fish and plants have a symbiotic interaction that is the foundation of aquaponics. Ammonia, which can be toxic to fish in high doses, is abundant in the excrement that fish create. But in an aquaponic system, ammonia is converted by helpful bacteria into nitrites and nitrates, which plants easily absorb. These nitrates are then utilized by the plants as nutrients, effectively filtering and purifying the fish's water. Fish and plants can coexist in a healthy ecosystem created by this nutrient exchange cycle.

A grow bed, a water pump, a biofilter, and a fish tank are the main parts of an aquaponic system. The fish are housed in a tank that offers a controlled environment for their development and procreation. The beneficial bacteria that carry out the nitrification process reside in the biofilter, frequently packed with a media such as gravel or clay pellets. The plants are grown in a bed that can be set up in several ways, including deep water culture, flood-and-drain, or vertical towers. Water is constantly exchanged between the grow bed and the fish tank via the water pump, preserving water quality and facilitating nutrient exchange.

Comparing aquaponics to conventional agricultural techniques reveals several benefits. First off, compared to soil-based agriculture, it uses much less water. In an aquaponic system, water is recycled and recirculated, so replenishing the water needed for plant uptake and evaporation needs to happen occasionally. Because of this, aquaponics is exceptionally well suited for dry climates or places with scarce water supplies. Second, aquaponics produces cleaner, organic produce by eliminating the need for chemical pesticides and fertilizers. By minimizing the risk of soil-borne illnesses and pests, the closed-loop technology lessens the requirement for chemical interventions.

Furthermore, aquaponics makes it possible to produce food all year round in any temperature or season. Growers may maintain ideal fish and plant growth conditions by installing the system in controlled locations like greenhouses or indoor spaces. This never-ending production cycle guarantees a consistent flow of fresh fish, veggies, and herbs, promoting food security and sustainability. Furthermore, aquaponics is accessible to hobbyists, urban farmers, and professional growers equally due to its application versatility, ranging from small home systems to substantial commercial operations.

Aquaponics has numerous advantages, but there are certain drawbacks that need to be considered to ensure successful adoption. Compared to conventional farming techniques, the initial setup costs of an aquaponic system may be more significant because of the need for tanks, pumps, grow beds, and other equipment. Nevertheless, long-term savings on pesticides, fertilizers, and water may compensate for these upfront costs. In addition, compared to conventional farming, aquaponics demands a higher degree of technical expertise and supervision. Aquaculture and hydroponics concepts must be understood by growers, who must also control water quality factors like pH and dissolved oxygen levels and guarantee the well-being and equilibrium of fish and plants.

Another critical factor in aquaponics is the selection of fish and plants. The quick growth rates, resilience, and flexibility of tilapia, trout, and catfish make them ideal for aquaponic systems. Nonetheless, local laws, consumer demand, and environmental considerations should all be considered when choosing fish species. Similarly, aquaponic systems are frequently used to cultivate leafy greens like kale, lettuce, and spinach because of their quick growth and high nutrient intake. Cucumbers, tomatoes, peppers, and herbs are all excellent options since they provide a variety of produce that may be sold or consumed.

To sum up, aquaponics is a cutting-edge method of producing food sustainably by fusing the finest features of hydroponics and aquaculture. Aquaponics is a highly productive, resource-conserving agricultural technique that establishes a balanced ecosystem in which fish and plants can thrive. It is an appealing alternative for modern agriculture, even though it necessitates meticulous planning, financial commitment, and technological know-how. Benefits include chemical-free products, year-round growing, and lower water consumption. Aquaponics has great potential to support food security, environmental preservation, and the creation of resilient agricultural systems as interest in sustainable methods grows.

CHAPTER XIV
Vertical Gardening and Space Optimization

Vertical gardening techniques

In places where growing space is restricted, such as urban areas, balconies, and small gardens, vertical gardening techniques provide creative ways to increase it. With the help of vertical surfaces like walls, fences, or trellises, gardeners can grow a more excellent range of plants in a smaller space. This section examines several vertical gardening methods, such as container gardening, trellising, and vertical gardens, emphasizing the advantages of each and the factors to be considered for a successful project.

Known by several names, such as green walls or living walls, vertical gardens are arguably the most visually arresting method of vertical gardening. On specifically made panels or frames fastened to walls or other vertical surfaces, plants grow vertically in these constructions. Fabric pockets, modular panels, or stacked containers are just a few materials used to build vertical gardens, giving designers and plant-choosing options endless possibilities. They are well-liked in urban settings with limited space because of their many advantages—such as increased insulation, reduced noise levels, and better air quality. Furthermore, vertical gardens increase biodiversity in urban settings by serving as a home for pollinators and beneficial insects.

Another proper vertical gardening method for supporting climbing or vining plants, like tomatoes, beans, cucumbers, and peas, is trellising. Trellises, which provide plants a structure and support as they climb, comprise vertical posts or stakes with horizontal supports or wires. Gardeners may boost air circulation, lower the risk of pests and diseases, and increase harvests by teaching plants to grow vertically along trellises. Fruits and vegetables are more accessible and less likely to decay on the ground when trellising, improving harvesting efficiency. Depending on available space and style preferences, gardeners can select from a wide range of trellis designs, such as straightforward A-frame constructions, arching tunnels, or intricate espalier patterns.

Another adaptable vertical gardening method is container gardening, which enables gardeners to cultivate plants in pots or containers affixed to vertical surfaces like walls, fences, or balconies. Because container gardening gives you total control over the growth environment—including soil composition, drainage, and water—it is perfect for tiny spaces and places with poor soil quality. Gardeners can design vertical gardens that fit their area and style using various containers, including wall-mounted planters, window boxes, and hanging baskets. Plant selection is flexible with container gardening, enabling the growth of miniature fruit trees, vegetables, herbs, and even beautiful flowers in small areas.

One of the most critical factors is ensuring plants have the proper support and stability when implementing vertical gardening techniques. Vertical buildings must be firmly fastened to walls, fences, or other surfaces so as not to collapse or sustain damage from wind, rain, or dense foliage. Furthermore, gardeners must consider how much weight their vertical structures can support and select the proper hardware and materials for installation. Regular care is also crucial to keep an eye on plant growth, offer assistance when required, and guarantee that plants get enough water and nutrients. Water tends to flow more quickly from containers or raised planters, especially in hot or windy weather, so watering vertical gardens may need extra care.

Choosing appropriate plants for vertical growth and growing circumstances is another factor in practical vertical gardening. Vegetables that climb or vines, such as tomatoes, beans, cucumbers, squash, and peas, work well in vertical gardens when supported appropriately. Ornamental vines, like morning glory, jasmine, or ivy, can also enhance vertical areas with beauty and scent. To ensure compatibility with their chosen vertical gardening approach, gardeners should consider elements like light exposure, soil moisture, and space needs while selecting plants for their vertical gardens.

In summary, vertical gardening methods provide innovative and valuable ways to maximize growing space in constrained spaces. With vertical gardens, trellising, container gardening, or a mix of these techniques, gardeners can grow various plants to enhance biodiversity and beautify their surroundings. Careful planning, appropriate support and upkeep, and selecting plants suited for vertical growth are necessary to implement vertical gardening successfully. By adopting vertical planting techniques, gardeners may turn ordinary spaces into colorful, productive gardens that please the senses and uplift the spirit.

Choosing the right vertical gardening system

Selecting the appropriate vertical gardening system can create a successful and fruitful garden in a small space. There are many styles and layouts for vertical gardening systems, each with benefits and things to remember. This section discusses several things to consider when choosing a vertical gardening system, such as the availability of space, the choice of plants, the level of upkeep needed, and personal preferences.

The amount of available space and the garden's placement are important factors to consider when selecting a vertical gardening system. Specific systems work well on walls, fences, patios, balconies, and other surfaces, whether outside or indoors. For vertical gardens in compact metropolitan areas or interior spaces with limited floor space, wall-mounted systems like modular panels or pocket planters are perfect. Gardeners may generate lush foliage in regions with limited ground space by installing these systems, which are simple to install on walls or fences.

The kind of plants you want to grow in your vertical garden is something else to consider. Certain plants, including ornamentals, succulents, veggies, or herbs, are better suited for particular systems. Whereas larger pots or modular panels can hold a broader range of plants, such as vegetables, flowers, and trailing vines, pocket planters with shallow pockets are perfect for growing herbs and other plants with shallow root systems. To ensure your plants will flourish in the chosen vertical gardening system, consider the mature size and growth habits of your selections.

When selecting a vertical gardening system, maintenance requirements are another crucial aspect to consider. Based on container size, soil type, and sun exposure, specific systems need more regular fertilization, trimming, or watering than others. In hot or dry conditions, self-watering or drip irrigation systems can minimize maintenance responsibilities by giving plants a steady water flow. It will also be more straightforward to care for your vertical garden over time if you select a system that is simple to access for planting, upkeep, and harvesting.

When selecting a vertical gardening system that fits your area and taste, aesthetic preferences and design considerations are important factors to get right. Think about the overall aesthetic you hope to accomplish with your vertical garden, whether a more natural, rustic style or sleek and modern. With the help of adjustable features like color selections, removable panels, and modular setups, many vertical gardening systems let you design a unique garden that expresses your style and individuality. Select a system that improves the visual appeal of your surroundings by considering your room's architectural elements, such as the lighting, colors, and textures of the walls.

The long-term effectiveness, weather resilience, and durability of a vertical farming system are important considerations. Select weatherproof, sunlight—and moisture-resistant materials appropriate for outdoor use. Seek for systems constructed from premium materials meant to endure the weather and offer dependable performance year after year, such as treated wood, metals, or weather-resistant plastics. You can also ensure you're investing in a reliable and sturdy vertical gardening system by reading reviews from other gardeners and considering the manufacturer's or supplier's reputation.

In summary, selecting the ideal vertical gardening system necessitates considering several variables, including available space, plant choice, maintenance needs, aesthetic preferences, and durability. By meticulously evaluating these variables and exploring available choices, gardeners can choose a system that fulfills their requirements and elevates their indoor or outdoor area. There are vertical gardening systems to fit any taste, budget, and gardening style, whether you want to produce a vibrant floral arrangement, a lush green wall, or a profitable food garden.

Maximizing small spaces

Maximizing small spaces when gardening requires strategic planning and innovative thinking to make the most of the available room for growing. You may employ many methods and strategies to create a valuable and lovely outdoor haven, regardless of the size of your balcony, patio, or urban garden. This section looks at a few methods for making the most of limited gardening spaces, such as space-saving methods, companion planting, vertical gardening, and container gardening.

With vertical gardening, you can grow plants upward rather than outward, making it one of the best methods to make the most of small spaces. You can produce luxuriant greenery in places without much ground space using walls, fences, trellises, or other vertical structures. There are many styles and layouts for vertical gardens, ranging from trellises and hanging baskets to living walls and pocket planters. They have many advantages, such as better air circulation, a more significant growth space, and a lower chance of pests and illnesses. Growing herbs, vegetables, flowers, and even tiny fruit trees in cramped urban areas, on balconies or patios, is made possible by vertical gardening.

Another method for minimizing space is container gardening, which enables you to grow plants in planters, pots, or other containers rather than conventional garden beds. Because containers exist in various sizes, shapes, and materials, you can tailor your garden to match your aesthetic and available space. Because container gardening gives you total control over drainage, irrigation, and soil quality, it's ideal for small urban settings. Many different types of plants, such as ornamentals, flowers, vegetables, and herbs, can be grown in containers. Additionally, moving plants around to take advantage of sunshine or add visual appeal is made simple with container gardening.

A gardening method called companion planting includes grouping several crops to make the most of available space, boost yields, and ward against pests and illnesses.

You can develop a varied and fruitful garden in a small space by choosing plant combinations that match each other's growth patterns, nutrient requirements, and pest resistance. For example, you may maximize space and give shade and support for low-growing crops like lettuce or radishes by planting tall crops like maize or sunflowers next to them. Moreover, companion planting promotes biodiversity by drawing pollinators, beneficial insects, and natural predators that enhance soil health and aid in pest control.

Space-saving methods like interplanting, square-foot gardening, and vertical trellising can increase harvests in small gardens. To provide more room on the ground and improve airflow, vertical trellising entails teaching plants to grow vertically along supports like stakes, cages, or trellises. By dividing garden beds into tiny, square-foot portions, square foot gardening is a technique for intense planting that enables you to produce a wide variety of crops in a little area. Interplanting is planting multiple crops together in the exact location to maximize the amount of space and resources available. For example, lettuce can be planted between rows of tomatoes or beans.

In conclusion, making the most of limited gardening involves imagination, preparation, and the thoughtful application of companion planting, vertical gardening, container gardening, and space-saving strategies. Whether it's a tiny balcony, a compact patio, or a small urban garden, gardeners can create attractive and productive gardens in even the tiniest of places by using these techniques. With correct plant selection, smart planning, and upkeep, a plentiful harvest of fresh herbs, vegetables, flowers, and fruits may be enjoyed year-round in small-space gardens.

CHAPTER XV
Creating a Green Indoor Oasis

Designing aesthetically pleasing plant displays

It is important to carefully consider elements like color, texture, height, form, and placement when designing aesthetically engaging plant displays to produce harmonic and visually appealing compositions. These design ideas can assist you in creating visually appealing plant displays that entice the senses and elevate your indoor or outdoor area, whether you're creating a living wall, a container arrangement, or a garden bed.

Given that it can elicit feelings, establish focus points, and create visual appeal, color is one of the most crucial design components for plant displays. To add depth and visual impact to your display, choose plants with complementary or contrasting hues by the color scheme you like to accomplish. For instance, combining cool-colored foliage, like blues, greens, and purples, with warm-colored flowers, like reds, oranges, and yellows, can result in a striking and captivating arrangement. To guarantee that your plant displays remain attractive throughout the year, consider seasonal color shifts as well.

Texture, the surface quality of leaves and flowers on plants, can give plant displays more visual interest and tactile appeal. You can add contrast and complexity to your arrangement by including plants with various textures, such as glossy, smooth leaves, fuzzy foliage, or spikey blooms. With coarser-textured plants seeming closer and finer-textured plants fading into the background, texture can help add visual depth and perspective. To create a visually rich and captivating composition, choose plants with textures that contrast or complement one another, keeping in mind your plant display's general theme or style.

Another essential factor to consider when creating plant displays is height, which can define space, provide focus points, and create a visual hierarchy. Plants of different heights, from tall, upright specimens to low-growing groundcovers, can provide movement and rhythm to your arrangement. When choosing plants for height, consider the size of your area and the surrounding features to ensure that taller plants don't overwhelm smaller ones or block views. Employ height strategically to guide viewers around the display and establish emphasis points. It will take them on a visual tour of the garden.

Form, which describes the structure and shape of plants, can enhance the overall aesthetics and design of plant displays. When choosing specimens for your display, please consider the plants' growth tendencies, including their branching patterns, general shape, and growth tendency. Plants with various forms, including cascading vines, spiky erect grasses, and rounded, mounding shrubs, can add visual interest and balance to your arrangement. To create a harmonious and unified design, consider the architectural characteristics of your room and choose plants whose forms reflect or complement those features.

The last step in creating aesthetically beautiful plant displays is arrangement, which is the careful placement of plants to produce visual balance and harmony. When placing the plants in your display, consider design elements like symmetry, asymmetry, rhythm, and repetition. You can add visual intrigue and movement to your display by grouping plants in odd numbers, arranging them in diagonal lines, or clustering them in drifts or swathes. Furthermore, please consider plants' inherent development patterns and provide them room to expand and thrive without crowding or fighting for resources.

To sum up, creating visually appealing plant displays requires careful consideration of form, color, texture, height, and placement to produce harmonic and visually appealing compositions. You may create gorgeous plant displays that accentuate the beauty of your indoor or outdoor space by carefully choosing plants with contrasting or complementing features and arranging them in your location. These design ideas can be used in garden beds, container arrangements, and living walls to produce visually appealing displays that enliven the surrounding space and stimulate the senses.

Integrating plants into home décor

Including plants in your home's décor is a great way to bring the outside inside, establish harmony, and improve the aesthetics and usability of your living areas. Regardless of the size of your home, there are many ways to use plants in your home décor to create calming and enticing spaces that support health and well-being.

Adding plants to existing furniture and accessories is one of the easiest ways to incorporate them into home décor. Put potted plants on windowsills, tables, or shelves to bring some greenery into any space. Select plants that blend in with your room's design and color palette by selecting ones with striking foliage or vibrant blossoms. To achieve a unified look, use ornamental planters or pots that match the rest of your décor. Additionally, think about using plants as organic accents in displays or arrangements. For example, gather potted plants to create a focal point in a space or place a vase of fresh flowers on a coffee table.

Another well-liked method of incorporating plants into interior design is hanging them, particularly in compact rooms with constrained floor areas. To add dimension and visual appeal to your location, hang plants from beautiful macramé hangers, wall-mounted brackets, or ceiling hooks. Select plants that trail or cascade, like philodendrons, pothos, or spider plants, to create a visually arresting display that draws the attention upward. In larger rooms, hanging plants can also help soften harsh architectural lines and provide a cozy, intimate feel.

Living walls, sometimes called green walls or vertical gardens, are a visually arresting and dramatic approach to incorporating plants into interior design. Plants are grown on specifically made panels or frameworks fastened to walls or other vertical surfaces in these displays. From little accent walls to massive installations that take up whole rooms, living walls can be made to match any design and size of the area. Select a range of plants with distinct hues, textures, and growth patterns to create a dynamic and colorful arrangement that turns your walls into living artwork.

Another inventive approach to incorporating plants into home décor is through terrariums and indoor gardens, particularly useful in areas with little natural light or access to outdoor gardening. Use a variety of plants, mosses, rocks, and other ornamental items to create tiny landscapes within glass jars, bowls, or cloches. Terrariums can be used to whimsical and charm any space when placed on tables, shelves, or windowsills. Use low-light-loving plants like succulents, ferns, and mosses to make a long-lasting and low-maintenance display.

Including plants in your décor makes your space more attractive and visually stimulating. Still, it has several positive health effects, such as better air quality, lower stress levels, and more productivity. By naturally eliminating toxins and contaminants from the air, plants create a healthier and cleaner indoor environment. Furthermore, taking care of plants can be a therapeutic and calming activity that lowers anxiety and encourages attention. Adding plants to your décor can help you design areas that enhance your general health and well-being and are aesthetically pleasing.

In conclusion, adding plants to your décor is an easy and efficient approach to creating hospitable and restorative interiors while bringing the beauty of nature indoors. There are many ways to incorporate plants into your home décor to fit your style and location, whether you hang them from ceilings or walls, showcase them on tables, shelves, or windowsills, or construct living walls or indoor gardens. You may design environments that are aesthetically pleasing, healthier, happier, and more peaceful to live in by incorporating plants into your décor.

Maintaining a balanced indoor ecosystem

Maintaining a balanced indoor ecology is imperative to creating a healthy and flourishing atmosphere for people and plants alike. An indoor ecosystem consists of elements that affect the general health of plants and their occupants, such as temperature, humidity, light exposure, soil health, and air quality. Achieving and maintaining a balance among these aspects calls for cautious attention and proactive management to ensure ideal conditions for growth and health.

Air quality is one of the most critical components of maintaining a healthy home habitat. Dust, allergies, poisons, and other pollutants can contaminate indoor air, negatively affecting plant and human health. And improve air quality, enough ventilation must be provided by opening windows, turning on fans, or installing air purifiers. Incorporating air-purifying plants, such as peace lilies, spider plants, and snake plants, can also aid in eliminating pollutants and poisons from the air, making everyone's indoor environment healthier and cleaner.

Maintaining a balanced indoor ecology depends heavily on humidity levels, particularly for plants that need particular humidity levels to flourish. While excessive humidity can encourage fungal growth and pest infestations, low humidity can cause dry air and plant moisture loss. Consider utilizing humidifiers or dehumidifiers to control the amount of moisture in the air to maintain ideal humidity levels. Furthermore, especially in dry indoor situations, clustering plants together or setting them on trays with water and stones can help boost the humidity surrounding them.

Another crucial component of keeping a healthy indoor ecology is controlling temperature since plants need a specific range of temperatures to grow and thrive. Most indoor plants thrive in daytime temperatures between 65°F and 75°F and nighttime temperatures that are somewhat colder. Extreme temperature swings can stress plants and hinder their growth, so keep them away from drafty windows, heating vents, and air conditioners. To control temperature and shield plants from extremes in temperature, use thermal insulation, curtains, or shades.

Because light is necessary for photosynthesis and growth, light exposure is essential to establishing a balanced indoor ecology for plants. Different plants require different amounts of light to thrive; some like bright, indirect light, while others do best in low light. Plants should be placed in your home with consideration for the natural light levels present, making sure they get the right amount of light for their particular requirements. Artificial grow lights, such as fluorescent or LED lights, can supplement natural light to give plants in poorly lit locations lighter.

Good soil is also essential for maintaining a balanced indoor ecology, as it gives plants the necessary nutrients and support to develop. Use premium potting mixes or soils designed primarily for indoor plants; these blends will provide enough aeration and drainage for the roots. To keep the soil equally moist but not overly wet, check the moisture content of the soil regularly and water the plants as needed. Additionally, to restore nutrients and promote healthy growth, fertilize plants regularly with balanced liquid or granular fertilizers.

In summary, a healthy indoor environment necessitates considering several variables, such as temperature, humidity, light exposure, soil health, and air quality. By setting the ideal plant development and health circumstances, you may enjoy a lush and healthy indoor garden while encouraging a cleaner and healthier atmosphere for your family. With proper maintenance and management, you can sustain a healthy indoor ecology that promotes the well-being of people and plants for many years.

CONCLUSION

Finally, for anyone wishing to start the fulfilling path of indoor gardening, "Indoor Gardening Essentials: The Complete Guide to Growing Plants Inside Your Home" provides an extensive and priceless resource. Regardless of expertise level or space constraints, readers have found the fundamental information and helpful advice required to create successful indoor gardens inside the pages of this book. By demystifying indoor gardening and offering concise, detailed directions, this guide enables readers to bring the beauty and advantages of nature indoors.

"Indoor Gardening Essentials" clarifies and explains every facet of indoor gardening, from choosing the best plants and containers to learning vital care procedures and solving typical issues. The readers now know how to evaluate their area, evaluate lighting and environmental factors, select appropriate plants, and confidently take care of them. To maximize their success with indoor gardening, they have also learned space-saving methods, creative design ideas, and inventive solutions.

With the knowledge and abilities found in this book, readers will be well-equipped to design rich, colorful, and flourishing indoor gardens that improve their living environments and make them happier. Readers can confidently and enthusiastically set out on a beautiful and happy indoor gardening adventure with "Indoor Gardening Essentials" as their trusted guide."

Thank you for buying and reading/ listening to our book. If you found this book useful/ helpful please take a few minutes and leave a review on the platform where you purchased our book. Your feedback matters greatly to us.

9 798330 205271